MW01090014

RESPECT
Your Children

A PRACTICAL GUIDE TO
EFFECTIVE PARENTING

JAY SCOTT FITTER
LICENSED FAMILY THERAPIST

iUniverse, Inc.
New York Bloomington

iUniverse books may be ordered through booksellers or by contacting:

iUniverse
1663 Liberty Drive
Bloomington, IN 47403
www.iuniverse.com
1-800-Authors (1-800-288-4677)

Because of the dynamic nature of the Internet, any Web addresses or links contained in this book may have changed since publication and may no longer be valid. The views expressed in this work are solely those of the author and do not necessarily reflect the views of the publisher, and the publisher hereby disclaims any responsibility for them.

ISBN: 978-1-4502-2066-8 (sc)
ISBN: 978-1-4502-2068-2 (dj)
ISBN: 978-1-4502-2067-5 (ebook)

Printed in the United States of America

iUniverse rev. date: 03/22/2010

To Ann, for all of your support. To Scott, Jayson and Victoria, for the unique ways that you contributed to this book. Thanks Jenna.

Contents

1	**Introduction**	**1**
2	**Communication Skills**	**5**

Patterns	6
Long Term Effects	7
Finding the Path	7
Children Should Be Seen AND Heard	8
Reap the Rewards	8
Communication Basics	9
Let's Talk About It	9
Age Affects Information	10
Role Modeling	10
Taking Time to Explain	11
You Can't Un-ring the Bell	12
Saying Sorry	13
Non-Verbal Communication	13
Listening Skills	13
It's Good to Talk....	18
Children Are Not Therapists	18
Final Thoughts	19
Assignment—Family Circles	19

3	**Discipline vs. Punishment**	**23**

Punishment Hurts	23
Discipline Helps	27
Consequences	29
Time Outs	31
Stop Rewarding Negative Behavior	32
Saying No to Temper Tantrums	33
Extinguishing Negative Behaviors	35

Positive Reinforcement   35
Customizing Discipline for Each Child   37
Be on the Same Team as Your Partner   37
Bottom Line   38

4 Parenting Newborns   39
Touch is Critical—a Lesson Learned the Hard Way   40
Lessons Learned   40

5 Parenting Young Children   41
Not Just Quality Time   41
Going to School   45
Mistakes Are Okay   46
No Wrong Feelings   47
Goal Setting   50
Active Parenting   51
Trust vs. Safeguarding   52
School Is Not the Ultimate Authority   53
Sharing Values   54
Supervision Is Needed!   54
Keeping Your Child Safe   55

6 The Teenage Years   59
Pick Your Battles   59
Space, Boundaries, and Privacy   60
"For the Fourth Time!"   61
What an Embarrassment!   62
Striving for Independence   62
Rules and Expectations   63
You Don't Own Your Children   65
Hugs   65
Give Your Teen a Way Out   66
The Importance of Socializing   66
Online Communities   67
Sexting   67

Clothing Trends	69
Change is a Red Flag	71
Academics & Temptations	71
Girlfriends/Boyfriends	72
The P word—Pornography	73
A Rite of Passage—From Child to Adulthood	74

7 Issues — 75

Nature vs. Nurture	75
Denial	76
Eating Disorders	77
Depression	79
Self-Mutilation	80
Date Rape	80
Sexually Transmitted Diseases	81
Drug & Alcohol Abuse	83
Dating	84
Teen Pregnancy	85
Peer Pressure	85
Abuse	86
Anger Management	87
Becoming Desensitized to Violence	87
Gangs	89
Helping Your Child with a Tough Situation	90
Education	90
Step-by-Step	91
Rebellion	92

8 Role Modeling — 95

Nurturing Our Children	95
Kids May Look Elsewhere	96
It Takes All Kinds	97
Generation after Generation	97
Breaking Free from the Cycle	98

Modeling Values—Monkey See, Monkey Do   99
Unconditional Love   99
Relationships   100
Separation & Divorce   101
Love—Not a Feeling, but a Decision   101
Single Parenthood   102
Role Modeling Abusive Relationships   102
Modeling Effective Communication   104
Anger Management   104
Appropriate Actions & Reactions   105
Religion   105
Modeling Hobbies & Habits   106
Case in Point: Alcoholism   107
Family Time   107
Cats in the Cradle   108

9 Taking Care of Yourself   111
Staying Active   112
When Times are Tough   112
Aggressive, Assertive, Passive   113
Empty Nest Syndrome   115
Connect with Your Partner*   118
Managing Your Emotions   121
Respecting Yourself = Respecting Your Children 127

10 Conclusion   129

Author's Biography   133

1 Introduction

Raising a child in today's world is a challenging task. Kids don't come with instruction manuals, and no test is required to approve potential parents. So, it makes sense that many of us feel unprepared and unready for the task at hand.

But the job doesn't have to be quite so difficult. There are strategies and skills that can help the parenting process be more effective and successful for the whole family. At the center of these techniques is one simple idea—Respect Your Children.

As a licensed Marriage, Family & Child Therapist for over nineteen years, I have seen the full range of parenting strategies, and of course the results, both positive and negative. Moreover, through my experience in a private practice setting, I have worked with countless families to improve their home lives, as well as running an agency for foster families.

Of course, for some kids, the repercussions of a poor family life can reveal themselves in dramatic ways; I've seen this firsthand in the past ten years, helping "at risk" adolescents who have unfortunately lost their way, resulting in a spell at juvenile hall or various residential facilities.

Furthermore, as a parent myself, with two older teenage sons in college, and a younger daughter still at home, I know that being a parent is the most demanding job in the world; one that we're proud to have, but difficult nonetheless.

Each one of us faces different challenges as a parent. Whether it's the entire idea of being a parent that you find intimidating, or you need help dealing with a specific crisis or issue, that's often what brings people to my door. Discipline, anger management, or even improving your marriage—I have taught courses on all of these topics for over fifteen years, and now I'd like to help you and your children establish a healthier family environment in your own home. These are skills and strategies that actually work; I use them myself and recommend them to parents that I meet every day.

Naturally, it goes without saying that building a happy home and learning to parent are all part of an ongoing process. As parents, we're continually discovering and developing new strategies to address new challenges as they arise, myself included.

But, regardless of your personal situation or circumstances, I believe that we all need to parent our children from a perspective of **respect**.

> **respect:** (verb)
>
> 1. to have an attitude of esteem towards
>
> 2. to pay proper attention or consideration to
>
> *~Collins English Dictionary*

So, what does it mean to Respect Your Children? It's about communicating with our kids, talking to them and listening to their answers. It's caring for them with love, instead of obligation or resentment. Whether it be discipline or simply chatting on the couch, parents need to tackle every situation from a position that starts with this one overriding principle— **respect**.

Now, giving respect doesn't mean that you are relinquishing your position of authority in the parent-child relationship. This is really about changing the way you *see* your children. It's time to start viewing your kids as people, not as objects or possessions.

As parents, we need to stop treating our children as less than equal—they are people, even though you have a parental authority over them, so you should start treating them how you would hope others will treat them. By establishing these positive patterns, they will carry on and not only benefit your children but also your grandchildren.

Respect is something that most of us demonstrate regularly, everyday, in the workplace. For example, many adults find it easy to show respect for their boss, despite the fact there is little personal investment in this relationship other than a paycheck. Yet, consider the sacrifice you would make for your child—you would die for them; you would give up anything to make your kids safe and healthy. If this is true, then why do you choose to show respect to a co-worker but not to the child whom you love more than anything?

Similarly, many parents demonstrate respect, kindness, and patience towards their child's friends, yet fail to apply the same politeness towards their own offspring. It's time that we start applying these respectful behaviors that we're completely capable of towards our own family on a daily basis. You may even find that you receive the same respect in return!

So, this book is about building this mutual respect, and it begins with creating a home where a child feels safe and secure, instead of walking on eggshells or feeling anxious. Even if you've had a bad day, your kids need to know that they are not your emotional or physical "punching bag" that you can take out your frustration on.

And it can start with something small. For example, if the television is too loud, you don't need to yell curtly, "Turn down that damn TV!" Instead, try explaining to your child that you'd like the volume turned down; treat them like a human being, not like a second-class citizen. Talk *to* them, not *at* them.

Parenting is also about being a good role model, not trying to be your child's "best friend." Throughout the course of this book, I'll share with you a variety of tools, skills, and strategies to help you become a better role model and a better parent.

Ultimately, this book will help your family become a better family—and it all starts with respect. Although there isn't a quick-fix or a band-aid solution, and there is no "one way" to parent your children, if you approach the job of parenting from a perspective of respect, you're laying the groundwork for a healthier, happier home.

2 Communication Skills

Communication is the cornerstone of all relationships—it is the foundation of how we interact with each other. Nothing could be more important than improving these skills, as it is communication that makes or breaks your relationship with your child. It's how you speak with your child, your ability to listen to them, and all the non-verbal cues you give them every day.

Therefore, it's no surprise that strong communication skills are the key factor in how this relationship between parent and child develops.

The good news is—these are skills that can be learned. And, with some practice, you can improve the way you communicate. Plus, with more effective communication, you'll also notice that other issues and challenges that arise in your household will become more manageable and easier to navigate. Let's start with a scenario that will be familiar to most parents:

~ Picture this

A youngster has just come home from school, and is clearly excited. "Mom, I scored this awesome goal in soccer today!" he says.

Mom replies: "Good for you, but why didn't you make your bed this morning?"

> The real message that Mom just gave her child was: "What's important to you is not really important to me. I've heard what you've said, but I'm not interested."

Even though the majority of parents never blatantly state, "I really don't care what you have to say," their non-verbal communication to their child tells them exactly that. And, over time, kids begin to read between the lines—a child feels rejected by their parent, because Mom or Dad has ignored and snubbed their dreams and interests.

What if instead, the mother had replied, "Wow! That sounds exciting. Tell me about it. What happened?"

This would have given the child a clear message—what's important to him is also important to his mom. (And, afterwards, at a more appropriate time, she could still make her point about his messy bedroom.)

Patterns

Now, everyone—myself included—has had one of those busy days, where everything seems to be piling up and you simply can't get on top of things. Of course, there will be times when you can't give your undivided attention to your little ones, so you needn't worry about "brushing off" your child once or twice, as it isn't going to destroy them. However, if this becomes an ongoing pattern, and routinely a parent is "too busy" for their child, there are significant consequences.

When a pattern persists, children learn that their parents are unavailable and begin to drift away from them. For instance, a child may see that Dad is usually busy when he's home, or Mom is seldom home. In time, they will come to understand that this parent is not someone they can turn to. And, if this is the established pattern, a child will often think that their parent is not interested in what they have to say and that whatever they want to speak about is not that important anyway.

Unfortunately, when a parent finally clues in, it's typically too late. Their child is often older and getting into trouble, and the communication lines have been lost. Because your child has previously learned that you weren't available, they have since found other ways to solve their problems and answer their questions. Thus, they aren't very interested in sharing and discussing their life with you; after all, they're simply following the pattern of communication you established when they were younger.

Long Term Effects

As parents, we're often very good at showing interest and communicating with our children when they're toddlers. For example, when your youngster brings you their newly painted picture, you gush over it, pinning it on the fridge with genuine pride. Yet, as time goes on, priorities shift and those paintings become the norm; you lose interest, or simply don't have time to talk with your child. All too quickly, we begin breaking down those lines of communication.

These lines of communication can be so easily destroyed. Usually, by early elementary school, many parents have already started to damage the fragile connections between them and their kids. Your child has so many things they want to share with you and tell you, but many parents claim that they don't have the time to hear about these silly, little things, that—to us adults—appear insignificant. But, from a child's perspective, this is big news, or an exciting discovery. They're running home to tell you and to share this with you. Nevertheless, if you don't accept them and their interests, that sense of trust and willingness to share with you will slowly disappear.

We can't afford to let these lines of communication break down. We need to develop and foster an open dialogue between ourselves and our kids early on, to lay the groundwork for later in life, and the troublesome teenage years. Ultimately, if we start early and work on it together, good communication is an achievable goal.

Finding the Path

Consider the pathway you and your child will be forced to take, if they feel like they've been turned away and rejected by you, time after time. Imagine this scenario—your youngster is a few years older and they've been told that a girl likes them. In a family with open lines of communication, the boy might say, "Hey Dad, there's a girl that likes me at school," initiating a conversation on the topic. However, if the child has been shunned every time something was important to them, it's probable that the parents won't ever hear about this new girl.

Nobody likes to be rejected, because it hurts. And, when it happens over and over again, it's a natural defense mechanism to emotionally protect ourselves. To a child, this means that they'll stop sharing things that are on their minds, for fear of being hurt once more.

> ### ~ Consider this
>
> *A man tells his wife, "I love you." But, every time he does, she turns away and groans, "Yes, I know." Eventually, the man is going to stop sharing his feelings of affection with his wife, because her reaction leaves him feeling nothing but empty and rejected.*

Children Should Be Seen AND Heard

Fortunately, keeping these lines of communication open with your child isn't rocket science. Simply, you need to take the time to listen to what they have to say and respect their ideas. That way, they'll continue wanting to share their thoughts and feelings with you.

Long gone are the days where children should be seen and not heard; this destructive adage helps neither the parents nor the child and does little to encourage a healthy dialogue between both sides.

Reap the Rewards

Of course, every now and then there are a few pleasant surprises along the way in parent-child relationships that have maintained these open lines of communication. Aside from being actively involved in their lives and helping them traverse the tricky passageway to adulthood, your child will also be able to share their successes with you, too.

For example, a young man (my son) recently called home while away at college. It was the middle of the day, and the father (me) wasn't expecting to hear from him. "Dad, guess what?" said the young man, "I just got back my chemistry mid-term and I got a B!" he continued, overjoyed.

Over the years, the father had supported his son and taken an interest in all areas of his life—academics, sports, girls; the young man knew that if it was important to him, it was also important to his father. Thus, he knew his dad would want to hear about this latest news.

As a result, both father and son were able to express themselves and share this moment together. But, it was a long journey to get here, and this level of communication and respect wasn't built overnight.

~ Advice is cheap

Anybody can give advice, but it doesn't carry a lot of weight if that's all you have to offer your child. If you establish a relationship built on listening, communication, and educated information, your children are actually going to want your feedback and input.

Communication Basics

So, we've established that parents need to take an interest in what their children have to say. We need to value and respect their opinions, and work to establish open lines of communication early on.

There's more to it than that, though. Let me share some of the communication basics, which will help you develop and improve your communication with your children.

Let's Talk About It

It's crucial that you don't make any topic "taboo" in your household, even sex. While many parents are reluctant to talk about certain issues, and are often uncomfortable discussing sex, your children are going to have questions. If your instinct is to change the topic when your child brings up a tough subject, fight that instinct and try to answer their questions no matter how embarrassing, awkward, or difficult they may be. If you don't answer them, or give them insights, they will go elsewhere for information or advice. Sometimes you may need to do some research, too.

So, be willing to talk about any subject, and let your children know that they can come to you, no matter what it is. Of course, if you've established or are working to create an ongoing dialogue with them, it should be easier for them to approach you and talk about situations or questions as they arise.

Age Affects Information

How we answer our children's questions is to some extent influenced by their age. This is likely something you've already done with your kids, as you probably speak to your children differently now than when they were infants. Yet, it's important to remember that we still need to edit and shape the information we give our children to create an age-appropriate answer.

For example—imagine a child asking a question about sex. Consider how you would answer an eight year old, as opposed to a fifteen year old. While both answers might mention certain elements of love and affection, you might not mention STDs to the eight year old, whereas this may be a key element in your discussion with a fifteen year old.

So, regardless of the topic, keep your dialogue age-appropriate.

Role Modeling

Communication is no different than other behaviors. Our kids observe and mimic the way we listen, share, and chat with others; consequently, it is very important to model good communication skills in your daily interactions.

For example, consider the way you speak with your significant other—it's highly likely that the way you interact with your partner will be how your child interacts with their future spouse and loved ones. So, your choices today will not only affect your own life, but also significantly impact the direction your children will take as they grow up.

— Being a role model: For better or worse

I recently worked with a troubled teen, who also happened to be a smoker. Among the many issues we worked through, the topic of smoking came up. We tried to encourage him to quit smoking and pointed out the many reasons for quitting, such as improved health and financial status. Over time, the teen decided that he would try to stop smoking.

And so, seeing that this choice made sense to him, he went home to his mother, who had always smoked two packs a day, and shared his decision with her. Wanting to help his mother, he suggested that she too should try to cut back the number of cigarettes she smoked. In reply she growled, "It's none of your damn business what I do. I'm fifty-two years old and I can do what I want." She didn't value or respect her son's opinion, regarding him as just a child, a teenager, so therefore what he said had no validity.

Interestingly enough, when I first met this teen, I noticed the same attitude resonating from him, dominating his interactions with others. Upon hearing of his mother's reaction, it became obvious that this teen had been simply modeling the poor communication skills he had observed from his mother.

Taking Time to Explain

Most children are inquisitive by nature, asking questions, wondering why and continually seeking new information. So, when they ask: "But, why do I have to clean my room?" many parents fall back on the old-school reply, "Because I said so." However, you should consider actually answering your child's question. (Though at times, children can be manipulative and will ask repeatedly, trying to assert control over the situation—we'll deal with this issue in the section on discipline.)

Try explaining, "Well, you need to clean your room because I want our home to look nice. We all have to do our part, and your room is your responsibility." By answering your child's query, you're showing respect, not giving in to them.

It's more than okay to explain your rationale to a child, instead of flaunting your authority with an absolute, "Because I said so." In fact, if this is the type of reasoning and communication skills you demonstrate, you'll quickly find your child mirroring this behavior when people ask them difficult questions, or even in a confrontation with a teacher. (They may even respond to you with this type of answer during their teen years!)

— A simple situation gone bad

A mother recently came to me out of frustration, for help regarding a conflict she was having with her seven-year-old daughter.

The woman explained that she had promised her daughter that she would take her to a pumpkin patch that day, once she got home from work. But she had to work late, and then run to the store before she got home in the evening. By the time she returned, it was too late for the two of them to go out. She told her daughter that they couldn't go and the young girl became upset.

"You told me we were going to go the pumpkin patch, Mom. Why can't we go?" the girl cried.

Feeling as if her daughter was being disrespectful, the mother sent the girl to her room.

The woman couldn't believe that her seven year old was expecting her mother to explain herself. What was the big deal?

I explained to this mom that as an adult, a pumpkin patch is not a big deal, but for a youngster, it was a pretty big deal. I also pointed out that she had made a promise to her daughter; however, if she couldn't do it, that was fine, she just needed to explain the situation. It could be as easy as, "I'm sorry, I had to work late, but we'll plan it for another day. How about Saturday?" This would have been a better reaction, instead of getting upset because her daughter was frustrated.

Again, this mother, like many parents, saw her daughter's feelings as invalid, simply due to her age. I reiterated that she and her child likely don't share the same list of priorities. But, just because something's not on our list, it doesn't mean that it's not on theirs, and we need to take that into consideration.

You Can't Un-ring the Bell

It's uncanny how certain things that are said seem to stick with us longer than others. Consider how many times someone can pay you a compliment before you start to believe it, and then consider just how quickly a negative comment can hurt you and stay with you.

The same is true regarding our dialogue with children. At times, all parents become frustrated. However, no matter how upset you are, you need to be careful about what you say, because you can't unsay it; you cannot *un-ring the bell*.

A child is always going to remember if you say, "I wish I never had you." Of course, the parent will apologize afterwards, but you simply can't take it back. Though we all make mistakes, as parents, we need to be cautious and selective with any negative words or phrases that may come back to haunt us.

Saying Sorry

With so many misconceptions out there, it's easy to forget that's it is okay to apologize when we do something or say something wrong. It's not a sign of weakness.

For instance, if you overreacted with your child, tell them. "Yesterday I was in a poor mood and I think I overreacted a little bit. It wasn't really because of anything you did; I was just frustrated with other things and had a lot on my mind. I'm sorry I reacted that way to you." You're taking responsibility for your choices, and owning up to poor behaviors.

By apologizing, you're modeling this skill to your children—it's okay to say you're sorry. In return, you're teaching them that they can do the same thing with their peers, with their teachers, and with you.

Non-Verbal Communication

Regardless of what you *say* to your child, often your non-verbal messages speak louder than words. We've all given and received these types of communication—crossing your arms when you're upset, furrowing your brow when angry, making eye contact when you're interested, or even yawning when you're disinterested. In fact, non-verbal communication is a bigger part of communicating than verbal communication.

Our body language speaks volumes without us even opening our mouths. For example, if someone is listening to a story, but rolls their eyes as you're talking, then the listener doesn't have to say anything in response—you know exactly what they're thinking! And, even if they ask you to keep going with your story, it's obvious that they're not genuinely interested in hearing what you have to say.

We need to be aware of this when speaking with our children; they pick up on these signals, too.

Listening Skills

What we hear is not necessarily what someone is saying.

What we say is not necessarily what someone is hearing.

How to listen effectively is a skill that many of us were never taught. For the most part, people nod and smile when someone is speaking with them, and if they're interested in the subject matter, they pay attention; if not, the listener merely "tunes out."

Unfortunately, often when one person is talking, the other person is thinking only about what they're going to say next. But, with your children, there is a more effective way to listen to them; a way which encourages your child to share and conveys to them that you're interested in what they have to say.

— Listening means focusing

Effective listening begins with focus—giving the person you're listening to 100% of your attention. That means turning off the TV, putting down the paper, maybe even turning off your cell phone. Instead of giving the other person a non-verbal message of indifference, right away you're saying that you respect them and are interested in their words.

However, if you're genuinely busy, multitasking like many parents, it's okay to tell your child that you'll speak with them later. "You know Sally, what you want to talk about is really important to me, and I want to give you all of my attention. But, right now, I'm doing a bunch of different things, so can we talk in about an hour?"

While that might seem like you're ignoring your child, as long as you have that chat in an hour's time, it's actually better than giving them only a fraction of your attention. Your child will realize that you really want to hear what they have to say and look forward to your discussion.

— Active listening

It's time to learn how to listen!

First, make eye contact with your child. Not staring, but eye contact.

Next, look at your body language. You want to tell your child you're interested by how you hold yourself. Crossed arms, leaning away from them; you are not going to send the right message. Try leaning towards them a bit if you're sitting down, or turn your body to face them; this says "I'm interested."

Now, the actual conversation: When someone makes a statement, it's tempting to simply reply with advice or an opinion, but resist this temptation. At the start of a conversation, this type of answer would simply shut down your child's openness. Instead of closing the conversation, our ultimate goal is to learn more about their situation, encouraging them to open up to us.

I like to use the analogy of an onion—their first statement is the outside layer. As a parent, you're trying to peel back the layers, to find out more about your child.

So, instead of stopping the conversation with a statement of your own, you want to *paraphrase* what your child said to you. Now, paraphrasing is not repeating word for word what they've said; it's saying their idea, the same message, but in *your* own words, telling them what you've heard. This lets them know that you've actually understood what they've said—this is the first layer of the onion.

For example:

> Billy: I had a tough day at school, Dad.
>
> Dad: Oh. Things didn't go well in class?

In this example, Dad's encouraging Billy to tell him more, but without saying, "Tell me everything!" It lets the child go deeper, without feeling like their parent is probing for information.

> Billy: Ya. There's this one teacher. She's so mean.
>
> Dad: She's kind of being hard on you, huh?

Each statement in this stage of active listening paraphrases back to the child their statement, which reiterates that you're listening to what they have to say and that you care. And with every new statement, the parent learns a little more, revealing another layer of the onion.

> Billy: Well, she wanted me to do this assignment and I did it, but then she said it wasn't good enough!
>
> Dad: Oh, she expected you to do a little bit better than you did?
>
> Billy: Ya, and I felt like I did the best I could....

At this point, the parent could say one of two things, either:

> Dad: Well, you should listen to your teacher, she knows what she's talking about.

Or ...

> Dad: Was there something in the assignment that she didn't like?

The first response ends the conversation with a statement; the child is not going to say any more. Whereas the second response continues the dialogue with his child. Remember, now is not the time to give advice—listening is not giving advice.

In fact, at this stage of listening, it's crucial that you don't judge your child, or put them down. These types of comments will immediately shut down the lines of communication. Also, you want to hold back any opinions or advice until they've finished sharing.

By listening instead of judging each statement, you're sending a message of respect to your child—you respect their ideas, their thoughts, and value what they have to say. They're receiving a non-verbal message that you care.

Thus, the paraphrasing part of listening continues until your child has finished expressing themselves.

> ### ~ Note
>
> Paraphrasing serves two purposes in listening. First, it helps the parent pull out more and more information from their child, but it also helps determine if you actually understand what your child is saying. For example, if you're way off base, your child can then correct you and re-explain what they were trying to say—without any crossed wires!

— Questions and feedback

Next, you can begin to ask questions. If there's something you don't understand about the situation, or there's an issue you would like clarification on, ask your child in a non-aggressive or non-judgmental way, such as, "Did you think about trying this ...?"

After any questions are answered, then is the time to offer your feedback, commonly known as giving advice.

Ideally, your child will have worked through the dilemma themselves in the course of your conversation; if no resolution has been found by then, together you can work out a plan or resolution. Often, your children will be more receptive to what you're saying, because they'll know you're both on the same page and that you actually understand what their problem is.

By helping your child to work through a situation, conflict or dilemma, the goal is that, as they speak with you, they will discover solutions on their own, and ways to better handle the situation in the future. Moreover, you're guiding them in the right direction, while simultaneously giving them the tools to reflect on the situation.

Naturally, sometimes the issue in question will involve hearing things about yourself as a parent. It's normal to feel defensive, but make an effort to listen to what your child is saying and consider their point of view. It's all about working together to find a solution.

> ## ~ *Did you know?*
>
> Research has found that, regardless of the type of therapy used, if a patient speaks with someone who *actively listens* to their concerns, issues and problems, they will improve.

— It takes practice

Like any new skill, learning to actively listen will take practice. For those who are completely new to doing this (and that's most parents), active listening often feels awkward or fake; you may also feel like you're unable to do it because it takes too much effort.

Of course, this doesn't mean that every time you talk to someone you need to be "actively listening." Sometimes a conversation is superficial in nature, and that's okay, too.

Remember, this will take practice and a fair amount of time to learn and master. But once you get the hang of it, it will start to feel more and more natural.

I often compare learning to listen with learning to walk. Initially, the child focuses all their concentration on trying to stand up and then they take a step. They wobble and then try to take another step, now looking for something they can grab onto for support. They're very focused because the task is both new and challenging, but as they practice and practice, it becomes second nature. And, as we get older, we can walk, talk, and chew gum, all at the same time, without even thinking about taking the next step forward.

Learning to listen is similar. Over time, it will also become second nature. If it feels different or unusual, that's normal. It doesn't mean you're doing it wrong, it just means that it's different.

It's Good to Talk....

When a child experiences something they see as traumatic, it's important that they're able to talk about the experience and work through it. This trauma could be something like being rejected by a girlfriend/boyfriend, or being teased and bullied at school, or struggling with a class. To an adult, we recognize that these experiences are part of growing up, but to your child they feel devastating.

With bullying in particular, children often don't want to tell their parents, thinking Mom or Dad will view them as a failure, a wimp, and someone who can't stand up for themselves. Therefore, it's important to encourage your child to talk to you about these difficulties. It might even be helpful to share a story of when you were bullied in school—how did that make you feel? How did you resolve it?

In the end, children need to be able to talk about the traumatic experience— so try and understand how they're feeling. As a parent you need to let them keep sharing and processing the experience until your child is ready to move on.

Children Are Not Therapists

It's important to remember though, that your relationship with your child is not an equally reciprocal one. While you're there to listen and guide your child, it is not an equal relationship; you can't expect your child to be able to use these same listening skills with you. Remember, you're not a therapist and neither is your child, so you shouldn't use them as such. Whatever their age, including teenagers, they shouldn't have to hear the problems that you're going through at work, with friends, or in your marriage; they're simply not ready for that developmentally.

However, people do need an outlet. But, instead of turning to your child, find another adult to confide in—be it a friend or a professional. There are also many different support groups available, too. Just remember, that while you need to be there for your children, helping them work through their issues, it's not a reciprocal situation, but you are never alone.

Final Thoughts

All of these communication skills have the same objective—to help you establish and maintain an honest and open relationship with your child. If you strive to build that rapport early on, practicing effective dialoguing and listening skills, you're laying the foundation for a solid, ongoing relationship between the two of you. You're also less likely to become that parent who says, "I had no idea they were involved with that!" (e.g., drugs, alcohol, questionable friends).

If you have open lines of communication, when your child is confronted with those types of issues down the road, there's a much greater chance that they'll come to you and share their questions and concerns. But, even if they don't, as a parent, you'll be more in touch with who your child is. Therefore, you will be more likely to recognize those types of changes in their behavior; ultimately putting you in a better position to help them, be there for them, and work through it with them.

As a role model to your kids, being a good communicator is key to a healthy and respectful family bond, one that will last a lifetime.

Assignment—Family Circles

Try this exercise with your family to help get a sense of how each of them views the family unit.

1. Everyone in the family takes a pencil and a piece of paper.

2. Draw a large circle on the piece of paper; this represents your family unit.

3. Next, using smaller circles, draw the members of your family inside the larger circle. Place those smaller circles anywhere you want, to show how you "see" the family. For example, if you see two siblings who are close with each other, place their

two circles close to each other. You will also want to add initials
inside these circles to help identify who they represent.

4.   Ask each member to explain their picture to the family.

It's important to let your child explain their drawing without voicing any
judgment, without trying to correct them, and without making them feel
guilty. Statements like: "Oh, that's not right," "You're way off base," "You
don't understand"—these are not helpful. Instead, take this opportunity
to ask your family about their pictures, and then let them explain it, in
as much depth as possible. If your child is hesitant, start with a simple
question like, "Why is Mommy's circle so far away?"

The objective here is to gain insight as to where you are as a family. You're
probably aware of how you see it, but this gives you a chance to see how
your spouse and children see it, too. Furthermore, this exercise creates an
opportunity to listen to how everyone else interprets family life.

Below are two different examples of Family Circles. There is no right way
to complete this exercise; however, if you're not sure, these should give you
an idea of what the end result might look like.

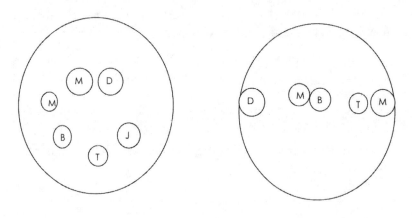

Family Circle 1   Family Circle 2

In Family Circle 1, Mom and Dad are close to each other, indicating they
present a unified front to their children, while the kids are a little further
away, but still relatively close. Mary and Betty are a bit closer to their
mother, and therefore positioned closer to her circle; whereas Jimmy is
closer with his father. Tom is further away from his dad, but only slightly,
and is still close to Jimmy.

In Family Circle 2, Mom is positioned on one end, and Dad is at the other end. Therefore, the child sees Mom and Dad as being really far apart from each other, and the kids are stuck in the middle of them. The one child who is closest to his mother may suggest that when Mom has a problem, she discusses it with this child instead of her spouse.

While many family circles are self-explanatory, I've included a list of some configurations, and what they may indicate:

- Two smaller circles, overlapping each other—this may indicate an unhealthy dependence on each other. Both individuals are "enmeshed" together; they're so involved with each other that it's unhealthy.

- A circle, covered in spikes—this usually indicates that the person is difficult to become close with; perhaps they're often hostile, rude, mean, or they hurt people.

- A small circle both in and out of the large family circle—this might show that that individual isn't home most of the time, or not actively involved in the family.

- Mom and Dad circles at opposite ends—may indicate that they're feeling that the parents are always fighting with each other.

Rarely are circles all the same. While some people may include pets, extended family members, step-families, others won't. Ultimately, look at this exercise as a starting point. If you're happy with how your family sees itself, that's great. If you're not, though, now is a great time to begin talking about some of those issues and improving your family dynamics.

3 Discipline vs. Punishment

Discipline is one of the defining elements of parenting; whether used sparingly or liberally, it's fundamental to the parent-child dynamic. Through discipline, children are taught to become responsible, honest, kind, sharing people. By following their parent's guidance, teachings, and rules, they ideally grow up to be well-behaved and respectful individuals.

However, if you *punish* your child instead of disciplining them, the end result will not be the same. Did you think that punishment and discipline were the same thing? Think again!

Punishment is an act of anger and impulse. It happens when a parent takes things personally; the punishment is, in fact, retaliation for the child's poor choice.

Discipline, however, is centered around helping the child, with the goal of correcting their choices and actions. A parent who disciplines is trying to teach their child right from wrong, helping them learn life skills.

Ultimately, punishment *hurts* a child, whereas discipline *helps* a child.

Punishment Hurts

The urge to punish comes from within when you feel hurt by a child's behavior—you're looking to strike back and inflict this same pain, often overreacting to the situation. For example, in the heat of the moment, Mom or Dad might lash out—even raising a hand to a child, instead of taking a deep breath and assessing the situation objectively.

The challenge if you use this type of authority is to detach yourself from the situation, and control your anger and impulses before responding or reacting to your child.

By controlling this anger and emotion, a parent can stop themselves from making the situation worse. And this is important, as punishment—which can lead to abuse—is usually both unreasonable and much more physical than discipline.

Most abusive parents never plan on hurting their child, but out of anger, they impulsively react and strike their child, punishing them with physical revenge instead of teaching them right from wrong.

— A slippery slope

Once trapped in this mindset of punishment, it is difficult for parents to think rationally or even compassionately about their child's actions.

And in an instant, on impulse, lives can change dramatically. A loving parent can be convicted of child abuse and land themselves in prison, simply because they impulsively did something violent to their child. If you choose to listen to your impulses and punish your child out of anger, you lose your self-control and your ability to think clearly.

Punishment is not an effective way to help your child learn. In fact, it is a dangerous path to follow. For example, a parent grabs their child by the hand. The parent is upset and twists the tiny arm. Being a "good parent" they take their child to the hospital to have it looked at—they find a greenstick fracture. The x-ray clearly shows how the arm bone was twisted. This is a red-flag for hospital employees who know this is a symptom of child abuse. In a whirlwind, Child Protective Services is called in, the children may be removed from the home, the guilty parent can be arrested and even go to jail. So, instead of reacting to an impulse, parents should use their better judgment and respect their children.

— Mismatched opponents

One of the biggest problems with an adult punishing a child is that the two are not equals. Yet, rarely does a parent focus on this inequality or the incredible vulnerability of their child.

But when calm and rational, no one would argue that children are the same as adults. They are not the same size, nor strength; they have less knowledge and fewer life experiences. Kids are unequal to adults in so many ways.

Furthermore, when parents punish their child out of anger, they teach kids that it's okay to treat those who are weaker, smaller, and younger with less respect. The parent is modeling a bullying type of behavior, which is obviously not a positive way to interact with others.

— Swats/Spanking

While I wouldn't recommend swatting or spanking your child, some parents may still choose to use this method of discipline.

Again, the match-up between parent and child is grossly uneven—the adult is much bigger, much stronger than a child. Children are easier to hurt than most parents think. Nevertheless, if you choose this course of action, for example, a swat on your child's bottom when they're little, I cannot stress enough—never do this out of anger. It is also important to warn your child beforehand so they understand that if the negative behavior continues, a spanking will be the consequence. This reinforces that spanking/swatting is the result of such behavior, not because they are a "bad person."

— Not a viable option

What I'm suggesting, choosing discipline instead of punishment, shouldn't be too difficult; in order to function in our society, adults must have a certain amount of self-control, impulse-control, and anger management. So these are abilities we all have on some level. I'm simply suggesting that these skills be used in our homes. It's a matter of respecting our kids as people.

Consider the dozens of interactions you have with others on a daily basis. Surely at one point or another someone has said something that you disagreed with, or they've done something that annoyed you. Yet, did you react by lashing out, or hitting the other person? Is there another situation where we, as adults, would act so recklessly, even if we were upset?

How many of us have punished our children out of anger? However, how many of us have punched a co-worker or slapped an associate across the face, because they didn't do a good job, they spoke out of turn, or they disappointed us?

In any other situation, you would react with a degree of self-control; otherwise, there would be severe consequences and you would be in trouble with the law. But, for whatever reason, some parents believe that with children, they have the right to hit them out of anger.

To justify their actions parents may say, "This is what happened to me, when I was growing up." While that might explain why you're more likely to parent this way, it doesn't excuse the behavior—after all, these same adults manage to function in society without violently attacking friends and other acquaintances.

So, instead of coming home and taking out your frustrations on your children, respect them. Certainly, your kids may do something wrong and increase your aggravation, but resist the urge to overreact and lash out at them. You'll only be doing something that you will later regret.

— What's the point of punishment?

If your child's safety isn't enough of a reason not to use punishment as a discipline strategy, consider the type of relationship you're developing with your child and the example you're setting for them in regards to problem solving.

If you use punishment, you're establishing a relationship with your child that is built on fear. If the parent is aggressive, vengeful, and unpredictable, the child will become very fearful of them. The youngster will worry about what their parent is going to do every time they make a mistake. Furthermore, this fear and anxiety will stay with the child later in life—like a perpetual worry, a concern about what's going to happen next, what the consequences will be for their actions. They will be waiting to be hurt, waiting for something to happen to them.

Moreover, by punishing your child, you'll be perpetuating this violent cycle of retribution. Your child will model this same problem-solving behavior with their peers and others. They will learn that if someone does something wrong, this is a suitable way to react—out of anger. Imagine what society would look like, if everyone functioned like this?

Obviously, punishment is not the best course of action for effective parenting as it's unlikely that the end result will be a respectful, well-behaved person. So, what's the point of going down this road? Instead, try respecting your child and teaching them through effective discipline techniques.

~ Picture this

A child is told not to bring their glass of grape juice into the living room. The parent took the time to explain how, if the grape juice were to fall on the carpet, it would leave a stain. But, the child ignores or forgets the parent's warning and takes the grape juice into the living room … and the youngster accidentally drops the juice.

In this situation, a parent who disciplines would react differently than the parent who punishes their child. *How would you handle the situation?*

Discipline Helps

Instead of punishment, parents need to become committed to disciplining their children. And, as the objective of discipline is to help your child, this should be in line with all parents' goals.

In its most basic form, discipline is a matter of choices and consequences. The parents explain their expectations for the child and should the child ignore these rules or expectations, there will be consequences. The aim of these consequences is to encourage children to stop negative behaviors, make positive choices and ultimately help your child become a better person.

— Where to start?

As mentioned earlier, communication plays a central role in your relationship with your child. When establishing discipline in your household, communicating your expectations and guidelines with your children is the first step. Initially, help your kids understand why these rules and expectations are important to you. Then, explain to them what will happen if these expectations are not met—what the consequence will be. By explaining to your kids the reasoning behind the consequences, you'll be helping them learn from their poor choices.

It's important that a child understands their parents and believes there is logic to their actions. Otherwise, not only is it impossible for the child to meet these goals, but if they break the rules, they have no way of predicting what the reaction will be. However, if everyone is upfront about what will happen, then your child will be more accepting of the consequences and parents are less likely to overreact.

Let's skip ahead to when your child does break one of the rules. All kids are going to test their parents to see if they will actually follow through on the consequences, so it's important that you remain consistent. Yet, when disciplining or discussing their consequences, remember that you need to remain calm, cool, and collected; this is not a time to yell, "Get to your room!" And, as the consequences should be pre-determined, disciplining need not be a stress-filled interaction.

The parent simply has to follow through on the consequences they've previously established.

For example, your teenager has been told they have 100 minutes of cell phone time a month. You explain that should they go over, they will lose their cell phone privileges for the next month. So, when the monthly statement comes in, showing that your teen has used 200 minutes, the consequence for this choice has already been decided. So, neither you nor your teen has any surprises.

Discipline is not about the parent being upset, or negotiating; it's about staying consistent, so your child learns that their parent's expectations are to be taken seriously. If the child chooses to not finish their homework or eat their vegetables, the parent simply says, "That's too bad. Unfortunately, you won't be able to watch TV tonight," or eat dessert, or whatever the consequence may be. Remember to notice when they accomplish these things, too—kids also need positive attention.

Discipline doesn't mean you don't love your child

Whenever you're disciplining kids, take the time to explain to them that you still love and care about them. Tell your children that they're not in trouble because "you hate them"; tell them you don't think they're a bad person. It's important to discuss with children, especially youngsters, that they've made a poor choice, and there's a consequence for their actions. But, at the same time, make sure they know that you still love them and explain how their behavior doesn't change that.

A parent's love for their child isn't something that should waiver—your kids need to know that. That way, when the discipline and consequence is over, together parent and child can sit down and talk about the choices and decisions that were made, with a goal to creating strategies that will help discourage these kinds of poor choices again.

It all comes back to the idea of respecting your children. Share your thoughts and ideas with your kids and, in return, they will share their ideas with you. Just because the topic is discipline doesn't mean that there can't be an exchange of ideas, or an open dialogue. Plus, by listening and respecting their ideas, your child will share with you their thoughts on the issues at hand, placing you in a better position to help them.

Consequences

Forming the foundation of discipline is the idea of choices and consequences; there are two main types of consequences—natural and logical.

Natural consequences

Natural consequences are those that happen whether we like it or not. Often times, these are outcomes that we don't want our children to experience; it's like learning a lesson the hard way.

For example, it's a cold day and your child chooses not to wear their jacket to school; the natural consequence to their choice is that they are cold throughout the day. Even if you told your child to wear their jacket, this consequence had nothing to do with you—it is out of your hands.

Yet, other natural consequences can be long term and quite serious, such as with a child's education. We can speak to our kids about the importance of education, but if they choose to put forth minimal effort, they may end up with poor grades and SAT scores and not be able to get into college. Further long-term natural consequences may also include struggling financially, or even difficulty finding employment. Again, as parents, we have no control over these consequences, and we want to protect our children from these experiences whenever possible.

For that reason, we continually try to guide our children in the right direction, encouraging them to make positive choices and decisions along the way.

Logical consequences

As opposed to natural consequences, where parents have no control of the outcome, logical consequences are decided 100% by parents.

In my opinion, the best logical consequences are directly linked with the actions, or poor choices of your child. For example, if you've told a youngster to put their toys away when they're finished playing, and they choose not to, the consequence would involve playtime and/or toys. Perhaps the child will lose a certain toy for the next day, or playtime may end early, to ensure the child has time to tidy up.

This is a great strategy for most issues that arise in a household. Although, it's important not to withhold necessities from your child, such as food, shelter, clothing, and love. For instance, if your child doesn't finish their dinner, withholding tomorrow's dinner would not be a suitable consequence. Withholding dessert, however, would be appropriate.

Whatever the case may be in your home, try to use logical consequences whenever possible. Discipline should always be appropriate and as immediate as possible, so that children, no matter what their age, associate the consequence with the poor decision they've made.

For example, if your child has difficulty completing homework on time, a logical consequence may be supervised study time for the next week. Or if their curfew is 10 p.m., and they return home at 11 p.m., a possible consequence would be reducing the curfew to 9 p.m. the following week. Explain to your teen that if they can show they're responsible and respectful of this curfew, it will return to 10 p.m. at the end of the week.

It's important, though, that you make the consequences realistic and for short periods of time. Otherwise, if your child has been grounded for six months, with no TV, computer or playtime, they'll likely feel pessimistic, realizing there's nothing left to lose, and the negative behaviors will return.

> ### ~ Possible consequences for your children ...
>
> *Remember:* When you limit or remove privileges, it should only be for a short period of time. This way your child will look forward to getting them back, and you'll also have the same tools in your arsenal if disciplining again in the near future.

For younger kids: Dessert, TV time, video game privileges, computer time, bedtime hour. All of these can be limited or modified as a consequence of poor behavior.

For older kids: cell phone time, car privileges, increased supervision, phone privileges, TV time, curfew, computer time or removing electronic devices.

Don't forget!—You never want to take away necessities that affect your child's safety, health and well-being. This includes food, clothing, shelter, love, etc.

Time Outs

Although they can be thought of as a logical consequence, "time outs" are often a standalone concept. Most of us are familiar with this idea; it's a very popular discipline technique used for younger kids. This is where a child who is acting inappropriately, i.e., hitting, screaming or kicking, is removed from the stimulation that's contributing to the negative behavior. The child sits on a chair or step that is positioned away from any type of stimulus, such as other kids or the television.

Ideally, this short break gives the child an opportunity to think about their actions and calm down, putting them in a better position to discuss their choices after their time out. However, it's important to keep "time out" time to a realistic amount. I recommend one minute of time out per year of age: e.g., a five year old would sit in time out for five minutes.

But, if a child is misbehaving even when in the time out spot, such as throwing a temper tantrum, the actual time out period doesn't begin until the child finishes acting out. To visually help the child understand, try using an egg-timer. This will help them see that their time out begins when they calm down; until then, the child will see that their official time out hasn't started.

— Time out for teens

Time outs can also be useful for teenagers, if, for example, there's a confrontation between parent and teen. Instead of sending them to a formal time out chair, have them take a walk or go into a different room to re-group and take a break. This should help alleviate some of the tension and aggression, giving both sides a chance to calm down. Note, however, that teens should never be sent to their room as a form of discipline—for many, this will be seen as a mini-vacation instead of a consequence.

— Parents can take a time out, too!

If you're a parent who used to punish instead of discipline, then this is a great tool to help you keep your focus and stick with the plan—disciplining instead of punishing. Or, of course, any parent who is shocked, stunned, or completely taken off guard by something their child does, can use this tool. Try taking a time out for yourself, before reacting and responding to your child.

If the situation is over, for example the incident happened at school, then after listening to your child's explanation, take some time to cool off and process what you've just heard. However, if the child is in the middle of making these poor choices, such as hitting or kicking another child in your home, take the necessary actions to make the situation safe before taking your personal time out.

By taking this step back from the situation, it helps ensure that you remain objective when you later discipline, as opposed to disciplining on the spot, in the heat of the moment, where you're more likely to punish your child.

Consider the parent who overreacts and grounds their child for a month. They have fewer tools to work with that month. Yet, if they don't stick to their discipline choices (i.e., two days later they tell the child they're no longer grounded), they're sending a message of inconsistency to their kids. In effect, they've told their child, "Don't worry, I'm not going to follow through with what I've said, so it doesn't really matter." Imagine the difficulties this parent will have the next time they try to discipline their kids.

Stop Rewarding Negative Behavior

Too often parents reward their child's negative behavior. This happens any time a parent initially says "no," but through their child's persistence and nagging, they eventually say "yes." This flip-flopping pattern is quickly recognized by children who, in turn, will use it to their full advantage time and time again.

Primarily, I see this when the situation has escalated, and children—usually two and three year olds—are throwing tantrums in order to get their own way.

> ### ~ Picture this
>
> *It's just before dinner and a child asks if they can have a cookie. Dad replies, "No, you can't have one right now, it's almost dinner." The child looks at the father and in a louder voice, repeats themselves, this time stating, "I want a cookie!" Dad stays firm and says no, but within minutes the child is now yelling, screaming, and jumping up and down, doing whatever it takes to get this cookie.*
>
> *Frustrated and irritated, Dad finally gives in and says, "Fine, have a cookie. Just be quiet!"*

In this case, Dad used a band-aid solution for a much bigger problem. In fact, what he just told his child was that if they throw a temper tantrum, they will get what they want eventually; Dad was rewarding the child's negative behavior.

Being a clever child, they will apply this technique in other areas, such as school, or in public, or in any other situation where someone tries to say no to their requests. And why wouldn't they, as you've taught them that eventually a tantrum will get them exactly what they want?

Saying No to Temper Tantrums

If you find yourself in this recurring situation, with a child who throws temper tantrums, don't worry—you can stop the cycle.

First though, you need to be prepared ahead of time. This is going to get worse, potentially much worse, before it gets better. Basically, there's been an unwritten agreement between you and your child—when they have a temper tantrum, you give in to their demands. Now, however, we're breaking this agreement and renegotiating the contract. Of course, they're going to be upset—they had a good thing going.

Let's go back to the cookie scenario. The child begins their tantrum with the expectation that their parents will eventually cave in and let them have the cookie; after all, this is what has happened in the past.

But instead, the parents continue to say no. So, the child escalates their behavior, doing whatever is necessary to get their parents to fall back in line and stick to the original deal. They scream, they cry, they jump about; the tantrum gets worse and worse. Stay strong and continue to say no. This is the hard part. Many parents will simply give in, because they don't want to deal with the tantrum any more. However, if you're prepared, then hopefully, you'll be able to continue saying no and mean it.

Eventually, the child will begin to see that their strategy is no longer working, and will stop the tantrum. If the parent is consistent, the child will learn that "no" actually means "*no*." If there's no payoff (i.e., no cookie at the end), the behavior will stop.

Of course, if you have been "giving in" to tantrums, it might take a while to make this new behavior stick. They may try it in public, in front of friends, or any other situation where they believe you're more likely to give in. But, it's about being consistent. If you continue to say no, you should be able to cut down on the frequency and drama of the tantrums. However, there is a small percentage of children who won't respond to these types of interventions and may require professional support.

~ Consider this

How many people put money into a slot machine, hoping it'll pay off? You may put one, two, or even a handful of quarters in, hoping you'll hit the jackpot. But, if there's no payoff, you'll eventually stop. Parents who give into tantrums are like these slot machines. A child will keep trying if they know it will eventually pay off.

— Teen tantrums

It's not just young ones that throw tantrums. Teenagers have been known for their dramatic antics for a long time. They may refuse to talk to Mom or Dad, or seek isolation in their room if they don't get their way. However, while their tantrums may look different from those of their younger years, by using the same basic principles you can extinguish their manipulative behavior, too. Consistency is the key to avoiding these types of negative behaviors.

Extinguishing Negative Behaviors

In addition to tantrums, there may in fact be other negative behaviors that arise in your home that you'd like to stop. If these are regular behaviors or habits your child has developed, using logical consequences may not be a suitable option. Instead, consider the motivation behind your child's actions.

Most children enjoy the attention of their parents. For many, negative attention is just as good as positive attention—it's still getting attention either way. So, if their motivation is to get you to notice them, withholding this attention will help stop the negative behavior.

For example, a child may continually interrupt conversations with silly, distracting behaviors. To stop these actions, simply don't give your child any type of reinforcement, either positive or negative. That means completely ignoring their actions—no laughing, no punishment, simply no attention given. Similar to the tantrum situation, if the child doesn't receive the expected pay-off, in this case, your attention; the behavior will inevitably stop.

If at some point down the road, the child reverts back to this unfavorable behavior, simply ignore it once again until the negative behavior ceases.

An important point regarding this technique is that it should be followed by positive reinforcement when the child does begin to act appropriately. This can be praise from you, or if suitable, a reward system can be created.

For instance, every time the child chooses a positive behavior instead of a negative one, such as sharing, not interrupting, using an indoor voice, etc., the child earns a token. These tokens can be accumulated and used for rewards such as ice cream, movies, or other pre-determined items. Of course, this idea can be modified to reflect the age and maturity level of your child.

Positive Reinforcement

Many parents consider discipline to be a negative consequence to a poor choice, but that is only one side of the subject. Positive reinforcement can be equally persuasive and is a great strategy for encouraging appropriate, suitable behavior.

The general idea is to catch your child doing something right. If our goal as parents is to have kids who are happy, successful, and productive, raising them to be good people who help others, who will be good parents and spouses themselves, then we should praise and reward them when they take steps and make choices that support this end goal. This way, kids will know they're on the right path, heading in the right direction.

As I've said, kids like attention, so why wait until they've done something wrong and there's a problem to give them this attention? Instead, of a negative consequence for *not* doing their homework, give them praise or a reward because they remembered to complete all of their assignments on time this week.

This can be especially effective if the child has been working on correcting a specific negative behavior. Talk to your child and let them know how much you appreciate their effort; tell them what a good job they've been doing and that you really see they're trying hard. People of all ages thrive on positive reinforcement.

And, people thrive on incentives. So, if you've noticed a change in behavior, you can say to your child, "Wow, you've been working really well on keeping up with your homework. Once you're finished, maybe we could go out and get an ice cream, or shoot some hoops together?"

Remember, spending quality time with you is a reward for most kids. You don't have to take them to Disneyland to win your child over. Simply take an interest in what they're doing and help celebrate their successes and positive choices, too.

Education is a great example, as young children rarely understand its importance. Instead of trying to explain it to them in depth, encourage their success by showing your interest in their schooling. It can be as easy as, "Wow! You've already finished that book. Great job! Tell me about it." You'll be reiterating to your child, through your interest, that school is important and that they're making good choices.

So, put some energy into giving your children positive feedback and catch them doing something right. It's a great investment in your kids, and will let them know they're on the right track.

Customizing Discipline for Each Child

Up until now, I've been referring to discipline as a blanket—one size fits all. But let me assure you, that's not the case. In fact, discipline is most effective when it's customized and tailored to suit your child's unique personality.

You may love your kids all the same, but that doesn't mean they all respond to the same type of discipline.

Consider your child's personality—are they emotional, sensitive, stubborn, argumentative, passive, insecure? It's important to figure out which discipline techniques will work best for each of your children, and which strategies will help them the most.

For one child, a stern look and a warning will ensure that the situation never happens again; however, with another child, increased supervision and loss of privileges may be necessary to convince them that their behavior needs to change.

Simply put—you don't have to take the same course of action with every child. In fact, the same discipline tactics that you use on one child might be completely over-the-top to use on another; and vice versa—one consequence may not be enough for the other one. Learn which techniques, strategies, and consequences work best for your kids; that way, your discipline will be most effective in helping your child learn the best way possible.

Be on the Same Team as Your Partner

You've seen it work on cop shows—the good cop, bad cop technique, but parenting is no place for this kind of strategy. Mom and Dad both need to be on the same page regarding acceptable behavior and appropriate consequences.

It comes back to the idea of being consistent. If a child knows that they can behave a certain way for one parent, it's very difficult to justify and explain why they need to act differently for the other parent. In most cases, this leads to the child manipulating the situation with the "good parent," making it harder for the "bad parent" to finally come home and handle the situation. Kids will "parent shop" that is, seek out the parent who will give them the answer they want to hear.

Furthermore, if you've positioned your partner in the role of the "bad parent," you're making their job of establishing a relationship with their kids more difficult. If you're looking to be the favorite parent for your own needs, this is simply not appropriate or healthy. These are your children, and you're here to parent them, not be friends with them while letting your spouse take the challenging role of being the disciplinarian.

So, ensure that both of you are equal and on the same page. As kids grow up, there are constantly new challenges to be met on the parenting home front. Make time to discuss your expectations with your partner, to confirm that you're both in sync.

"Wait until your father gets home!" is not the family motto I would recommend. Neither parent should be the bad guy. In fact, your child shouldn't even be surprised by the consequences. They made a choice, and they know that there will be consequences. And, if both parents are in agreement on the consequences, then your child will know that the consequences are real and should be taken seriously.

Bottom Line

At the end of the day, discipline is a fundamental part of being a parent. It is through discipline that we're trying to shape our kids into the best people they can be; hopefully they will respect our opinions and not just our authority.

Over time, as they grow, they will understand that what we're saying and doing is in their best interest; this discipline is out of love, and not out of revenge. It's done to help develop their character, and to teach them skills and attributes that will last a lifetime. As well, it will help them to become better parents to their own children one day.

4   **Parenting Newborns**

During the first six-to-nine months of life, children experience much of their world through physical sensation, or touch. This is how they explore their new surroundings and learn about the world around them.

Imagine their life just a few months before—all warm, snug, and worry-free in the womb. Once in the outside world, it can be very scary; as a result, babies need a lot of physical contact. By holding and massaging your infant, you can help them feel safe and secure. This will help them thrive in the first months of life, and it will also have long-term effects of feeling safe and secure later in life.

In their early weeks and months, babies may cry in an attempt to seek your loving touch. Please don't think that your newborn is being manipulative, or that you'll be spoiling them if you hold them often. Your baby is simply trying to communicate with you, and crying is one of the few ways they can ask for the safety of your arms or the comforting warmth of your body.

Infants need to be held in order to thrive and be healthy; holding them will help them grow, both physically and developmentally, gain weight, and move forward in all areas of their young life. Babies need more than to simply be fed; they need to be loved and nurtured.

Touch is Critical—a Lesson Learned the Hard Way

In the early 1900s, orphanages in the U.S. experienced an incredibly high mortality rate for newborns and infants, sometimes as high as 100%! Mystified, doctors and staff could not understand why the babies were dying. After all, these infants were given food, water, and what the staff believed were the necessities of life. But before many of the babies could reach a young seven months of age, an extremely high percentage of them died.

Moreover, every attempt was made to keep the infants clean and sterile, free from germs, in an effort to keep them healthy. To further this preventative measure, little physical contact was given to the babies. Sadly, it was this lack of physical contact that was the problem.

The healthy babies that did survive had only received one thing differently from those who didn't—the babies that thrived were given regular physical contact (secretly, by the night cleaning staff!) and because of this much-needed human contact, cuddling and play time, they survived and thrived.

So, just as important as air, food and water, babies need to be held. Without this physical contact—the rocking, the holding, the massaging—your baby will be undoubtedly adversely affected.

Lessons Learned

Even today, when babies are born prematurely and have an extended stay in a hospital's neo-natal unit; despite their fragility, they are regularly taken out of incubators and held, several times a day. Doctors have recognized the importance of this physical contact, stroking and rocking, and realize just how vital it is to the well-being of the baby.

Regardless of the risks, this "holding" is so valuable and necessary for babies to thrive. It simply can't be mechanically replicated. They need to be held, in an extreme sense, in order to survive. Thus, you should regularly hold your baby—stroke them, comfort them, help them feel safe and secure with your touch.

5 Parenting Young Children

Eventually, all of our kids will go through the toddler stages and work their way through elementary school, growing, changing, and developing as individuals. Much of our responsibility as parents is creating a solid foundation during these younger years, to guide our children in the right direction, instilling our values and beliefs at a time when they'll be open and eager to listen to us.

As most parents of a teenager will tell you, parenting tends to become trickier and more challenging as they get older. However, if you take the time to lay the appropriate groundwork during their younger years, the payoff will be both short term—with well behaved, happy, and healthy young children—and long term—with teens who will be more open to your values and listen to your point of view.

Not Just Quality Time

Most if not all parents would agree that spending time with your children is important. But, when faced with the daily struggles of running a household, providing for your family, and balancing everything else, too often it is time with our children that becomes lost in the shuffle.

We've all heard that it's important to spend "quality time" with our kids, and I completely agree. However, *quality* time is not a substitute for the *quantity* of time you spend together. For instance, a parent might say, "That was a great chat we just had together. I know it was only for ten minutes, but it was good 'quality time.'"

If this is the only time the parent and child have spent together all week, then it's simply not enough. Consider the hours your kids spend at school, with friends, or even watching TV. If a parent only spends ten minutes with a child, compared to the hours they spend listening to these others, it's unrealistic to think that you will have much influence with your child at all.

It's simply a matter of doing the math. Kids spend six hours a day in a classroom and on average receives less than ten minutes a day of one-on-one time with their parents. In which case, the time with peers at school completely outweighs the child's time with parents. For many children, the actions and choices of their peers will be their strongest guiding force, if parents haven't taken steps to adjust this balance by spending both quality and quantity time together.

For the child who doesn't have a parent speaking with them about peer pressure, listening to their struggles, discussing what appropriate choices are, it's almost impossible for kids to do anything different than their peers, whether it be acting out, behavior issues, sexual activity, etc.

— It's easy!

Spending quantity time with your children isn't rocket science. It's about finding simple, everyday ways to hang out with your child. It can be as easy as watching a cartoon together.

Although, if you like the idea of watching TV together, let your child choose the show. Many parents believe that if they're going to watch TV that they should be the ones to decide what to watch. After all, it's their home, their TV; they're the adult, so it should be their choice. But parents also need to be willing to sit down and watch the program their child wants to watch. Whether it be *Sesame Street* or *Dora the Explorer*, sharing that time with your youngster, respecting their choice of (appropriate) entertainment, is a good way to spend time together. This can also be a great time to share thoughts and ideas with each other.

Additionally, it's important to recognize your child's accomplishments. When they're young, this can be as simple as measuring and acknowledging their growth. To do this, place a measuring stick on the wall, and measure the height of your young child. Try measuring your child once a month, to see if they've gotten taller, praising them as they grow. "Wow—you grew a half inch since last month!"

Most children will grin as they hear the results, and thoroughly enjoy the positive attention you're giving them. As adults, we may understand that getting taller is a predictable part of growing up, but to a child, this is an exciting progress. Your child may even look forward to being measured and ask you to see if they've grown.

At the end of the day, it's about going out of your way to find and celebrate the accomplishments of your child, whether it is finishing a book, sharing with siblings, or even growing in height!

> ## ~ Ask for more info
>
> *Another simple success to acknowledge is when your child has a good idea. For example, when your child comes up with an idea for their new school assignment, ask them about it. "How did you think of that? Tell me about this cool idea...."*
>
> You'll be showing your child that you're genuinely interested in what they're doing and thinking.

— One-on-one time

Furthermore, if you have multiple kids, it's also important to have regular one-on-one time with each of your children. Again, this is one of those items that tends to quickly be forgotten or overlooked in the hustle and bustle of "real life"; for that reason, I strongly recommend setting up a routine with planned one-on-one times. This can be going to the park together, walking the dog, taking a child to piano lessons, or even getting a snack together. Regular one-on-one time provides your children with the opportunity to talk candidly and openly with you about anything they'd like.

It's simply not enough to always have "family time," where you only interact with all your children at the same time; often children will not want to open up and talk about a problem they're facing with an audience of siblings. If they're being bullied at school, have questions about the opposite sex, or even problems with another sibling, bringing up these issues in a group setting may be uncomfortable or embarrassing; it may be easier to just ask someone else other than you....

However, if once or twice a week, they know they'll have your attention and be able to talk privately with Mom or Dad, you're creating a positive and unique relationship with that child. Now I'm not suggesting a devoted "talk time," to delve into their lives, but more of a regular outing or activity for just the two of you, where they can talk about things that are on their mind, if they'd like to.

You'll likely find that with young children, they look forward to that activity, knowing it's their special time, just the two of you.

— Question period

Moreover, by establishing these regular one-on-one times, you're helping to create an environment where your child will feel comfortable coming to you with any questions, instead of asking their coaches, teachers, and peers, who may not share the same values and beliefs as your family.

For example, as kids start getting older, their bodies start changing, and often they have questions about these changes that puberty brings. They may be told one thing in school, another thing in the playground, and if they don't hear your thoughts on the matter, they may simply believe what these other sources have told them.

Of course, many parents are not comfortable talking about these natural changes with their child—they're often embarrassed themselves. But you need to take an active role, and the one-on-one time you spend together is likely the perfect opportunity. It can start with simply saying, "I've noticed some things...." or "Do you have some questions about what's happening?" or even "Let me explain some of this to you."

But daughters are not going to want to talk about this in front of Dad, and sons are not going to want to discuss this in front of Mom; and neither is going to want to talk in front of their siblings. As parents, we need to help our children feel comfortable with their bodies and these changes, providing them with the right information, in line with your family's beliefs and values.

> ### ~ Not up to the challenge?
> ### Consider the alternative...
>
> *A young boy discusses the changes he's experiencing with a few friends at school. They tell him it means he's now ready to have sex with a girl. With no further guidance from his parents, the boy starts becoming sexually active....*
>
> Sounds like the end results are worth having a few awkward conversations.

— Don't focus on your finances

Simply put—money is not a substitute for being there for your kids. Many parents, wishing to give their family a dream vacation, or expensive toys, think about taking on a second job. However, everything has its price ... and, the time you'll be spending away from your children has a very steep price tag.

There will always be families with more money, but spending time with your children when they're young is something you'll never be able to have again. As parents, however, we need to recognize that there's nothing we can buy that will ever take the place of being there for our children. Being a parent should be our first job.

Still not convinced? Consider the children who have lots of money, and everything they want, who still end up in all kinds of trouble, and accomplish very little in life. The bottom line is: you can give your kids everything in the world, but if you're not there for them, there are going to be behavioral and social problems....

Going to School

As I mentioned above, children spend a very significant amount of time at school; totaling on average thirty hours a week. With that being said; it's important to know what's going on at school, and if possible, become actively involved, by volunteering, joining the PTA, etc. When your children are young, they'll be excited and happy to have you volunteer—most will love having you help out in their classroom!

They typically have a big smile on their face when you walk in, and they proudly say, "That's my Dad" or "That's my Mom." But, this is a limited time offer; once your child reaches junior high school or high school, they don't usually want their parents involved anymore. So, while your child is young, seize this opportunity. All it takes is one hour a week; this gesture shows that you're interested in how your child spends their day, that you see what's going on at school, and that you're connecting with their teacher. In essence, this is time you're spending with them.

Of course, I understand that for various reasons, volunteering during the day will not be an option for every parent, and that's okay. But there are still school commitments that you need to be aware of and prioritize. One must-attend function is the Parent-Teacher Conference, which takes place at least once a year, when your children are young.

This conference allows you to get a clearer picture of how your child is doing in school—academically and socially. Often, parents will not prioritize this meeting, noting how busy their schedule is, but consider this: if your boss scheduled an important meeting on a certain date and time, wouldn't you figure out a way to be there? This is the same situation, only it involves your child. So, if in the past you've skipped this meeting, take another look at your priorities—you'll make it to a meeting arranged by your boss; why miss a meeting that focuses on your child?

Take the time to go; find out what your kids are learning, where they're struggling, and how you can help them. Unfortunately, so I'm told by elementary school teachers, the no-shows are usually the parents who most need to attend the Parent-Teacher Conferences, as their children are exhibiting behavior problems. Coincidence?

Mistakes Are Okay

With so much responsibility and so many different tasks at hand, being the "perfect" parent may seem unrealistic … and it is. Parents don't have to be perfect, so don't set unrealistic expectations for yourself. It's okay to make mistakes.

Our children aren't fragile and will recover if we make little mistakes along the way. In fact, if you're able to recognize that you have made a mistake, this can be a great opportunity to role model for your children that it's okay for them to make mistakes and own up to them, too.

For instance, if a child has done poorly on a test at school, but has seen that mistakes happen to everyone, instead of feeling down and dwelling on this upset, this child is more likely to regroup and move on, as they have seen that everyone can make errors.

> ### ~ Will this matter in five years?
>
> *Someone has made a poor choice, received a poor grade, or has not been successful at a competition. Before anyone overreacts to the situation, consider if this choice, action, or result will matter in five years time. Look at the big picture—are you even going to remember this mistake? Losing a swim meet will likely not matter for most kids in five years, but getting someone pregnant will definitely matter.*
>
> The same is true for parents—don't lose your cool if you make a poor choice or say something wrong. Mistakes are part of parenting; it's a learning process.

No Wrong Feelings

A key part of raising your child is teaching them how to deal with their emotions, work through their thoughts, and how to choose the best course of action. For some children, this is an easy process that comes quite naturally. However, other children may find that making "good choices" can be quite a challenge.

To help your child understand, process, and deal with their emotions, thoughts, and actions, begin by addressing the first response—their emotional reactions.

Initially, you need to encourage your child to express their feelings—and let them know that there are no wrong feelings. It's okay to feel angry; it's okay to feel upset and frustrated. All feelings are okay, whether you're happy, sad, joyful, discouraged, annoyed, excited, or angry. So, as parents, we should never tell our kids they shouldn't feel a certain way; a feeling isn't right or wrong, it just is.

Usually, to process our emotions, we begin thinking about the situation or conflict in more depth. This is different from feelings, because we're actively pursuing and working through an idea; we're taking it to the next level. And while there are no wrong feelings, we can take our feelings down the wrong path, in the wrong direction with our thoughts.

These thoughts, right or wrong, usually lead to actions—and there are definitely right and wrong actions. So, if your child is having difficulty directing their thoughts in a positive, constructive way, or regularly makes wrong choices, try to help them identify some warning signs, feelings, and thoughts that usually occur before these poor actions are made.

> ## ~ Warning signs
>
> *Warning feelings:* I'm feeling—angry, frustrated, hurt, confused.
>
> *Warning thoughts:* I'm thinking about—hitting somebody, hurting somebody, getting back at somebody, damaging something.

While these feelings are not wrong, these thoughts are warning signs. By helping your child recognize these signals, they'll learn that when they're thinking these types of things, that they need to stop those thoughts and work through these emotions in a different way. So, for a child who has anger issues, they'll learn that feeling angry is okay, but when they think about doing things to act on this anger, it's a warning sign that they're on a negative path.

The next step is to create appropriate strategies with your child, as that will help them deal with their anger in a healthy way. Your child may try: spending five-to-ten minutes writing about how they feel; get physically active, try doing fifty push-ups. For some, writing will be a good emotional outlet, while other children will benefit from physically exhausting themselves, leaving them with no energy to physically act out and harm someone. Furthermore, both strategies give your child the opportunity to "cool off" and think about their feelings and potential actions before acting on them.

If this is an issue for your child, talk to them to find out what their warning signs are; often it helps to work backwards from a recent poor decision. Ask questions such as, "What happened before you got in the fight? How were you feeling when that was said/done?"

Some people also have physical warning signs that can let them know that they are about to make a bad choice. Their ears may feel warm, they may feel pressure in their head, or they might start to twitch. Help kids recognize if they have any of these warnings signs as a way to stop them from making a bad choice.

By working through these emotions and thoughts, you'll be giving your child the tools they need to make better choices and take smarter actions.

— What would Oscar De La Hoya do?

Another reason a child may cite for getting into a fight is because they were challenged. "I couldn't back down, because then it would mean I was a wimp, or letting someone punk me." To help them understand that many strong, smart people would choose to walk away from this type of challenge, try this:

Ask the child who their favorite athlete is.

The child replies with Tiger Woods, Oscar De la Hoya, Michael Phelps, David Beckham, Serena Williams, Kobe Bryant, etc.

Then, have the child imagine that Oscar De La Hoya (or whoever they've said their favorite athlete is) is walking through an airport, and that same bully from school came up to them and challenged this superstar to a fight.

Ask the child, "What do you think Oscar De La Hoya would do?"

Almost every kid will know that the professional athlete would ignore the taunt and walk away from the situation.

Ask them, "Why would they do that? Do you think they're afraid of that person?"

Again, most children will know that that's not the reason. Many children will understand that this famous athlete would have big consequences if they got into a fight. They would get in trouble with the police, they might be sued....

So, as an adult, try pointing out to your child that they're right—this athlete would think through the consequences of their actions and realize that it's not worth it. You can then use this as a link to encourage your child to think through their choices before acting them out.

With this example, you can help your child understand how they can act just like their favorite athlete and walk away; walking away doesn't mean you're afraid, it means you're being smart. In fact, your child has just told you that this is exactly what really strong and smart people would do in this situation.

Goal Setting

It goes without saying that each child is unique and individual. Therefore, it's crucial that parents respect their child's unique goals, personality, and interests, helping them achieve and succeed to the best of their ability. For every child, these goals will be different, and our expectations will be different as well. But, as parents, we need to help our kids set and reach realistic goals in life—on personal, social, and professional levels.

Academic success is an obvious area for goal setting with young children. But even here, we need to remember that not all children have the same strengths in the classroom. One child will work as hard as possible, doing their very best, and end up getting Cs, whereas another will earn straight As with ease. We need to remember that either result is okay, as long as our children are doing their best.

But it's our job to help kids accomplish all they can be, and not become disappointed if they reach for *their* goals, instead of *ours*.... It's a common pitfall for parents—many try to live vicariously through their kids. Does this sound familiar? "I could have been a great lawyer, but didn't have the chance. Now though, my kid's going to become a great lawyer."

Instead, find out what activities make your child happiest, and help them set career goals that match. This may mean that they enroll in an apprenticeship or a trade school, instead of a top university—but that is still achieving a goal: a successful end-result. If this is their best effort, then it's more than "good enough," it's an achievement.

In the same breath, if your child is blessed with academic smarts, support them and encourage them to pursue their goals too, be it university, med school, or whatever the case may be.

At the end of the day, as a parent, our goal needs to be helping our children live up to their potential. Not sure what that is? When your child brings home their latest report card, or a class test, ask them, "Did you do the best you could?" If they answer yes, then you can reply, "That's great, I'm proud of you. You did your best." If they tell you "no," that this isn't their best, that they should have studied more instead of playing video games—then together you can help figure out ways to improve and adjust their study methods, such as increased supervision.

Ultimately, our goal is to raise happy, healthy, productive individuals who achieve their potential, no matter what that is.

Active Parenting

Parents need to take an active role in their children's lives, while still giving them an opportunity to develop and grow as individuals. Yet many parents find that striking this balance can be quite challenging. We're all familiar with both sides of this pendulum: on one hand, there are the families where children are seen and not heard, and these kids are monitored and scheduled every moment of the day; and at the other extreme, there are households where children are given free reign, and the parents believe that kids should "do their own thing."

Extremes are never the best route to go; in fact, it is somewhere in the middle where parents and children alike will find the best results. This means creating structure for your kids—routines, expectations, consequences, and guidelines for them, while still allowing them appropriate opportunities to make their own choices and express their individuality.

By giving children these opportunities to make some decisions on their own, parents are building a trusting relationship with their child. But, at the same time, through structure and guidelines, you'll also be providing a safe environment for them to grow. And young children, especially, need this structure to feel safe; they may not always like it, but it does give them a sense of security.

Although you may not hear young kids complaining if they're being asked to fend for themselves, what are we teaching them, if we're not there to help or support them? You'll be telling them early on that they must find this guidance elsewhere and that they can't rely on their parents to be there for them. This is part of the breakdown of the parent-child relationship, as your child will be forced to find other resources to answer the thousands of life questions they have.

— Appropriate options

So, what areas should your children be allowed to make decisions in? What are suitable issues where they can make their own choices?

Well, under your guidance, kids may be able to help make many choices that affect them on a daily basis. But instead of giving them endless options and opportunities to make poor decisions, start by giving them a few choices, such as, "Here are two sweaters, which one would you like to wear today?" Or, let them have a say in how they'd like to style their hair.

Again, though, parents need to be actively involved in the process. And being active and present for morning routines is paramount when your children are young. Countless children appear at school every morning, without having a suitable breakfast, bringing an inadequate lunch, or wearing inappropriate clothing. It's our job as parents to adequately prepare them for the day ahead—giving them the best start possible.

Eventually, your children will be able to do this on their own—but by then, they'll understand what your expectations are, what are suitable choices. It doesn't mean that they'll always make the right choice, but you'll have taught them, during these early years, what is expected and what is appropriate.

Consider the child that gets up alone in the morning, eating only a piece of cake for breakfast. If Mom or Dad hasn't guided them on what makes a healthy breakfast, they'll be choosing what to eat based on what tastes the best. The child isn't thinking of the long-term consequences of an unhealthy diet, or the short-term consequences of the sugar high and low that will affect their energy levels throughout the school day.

So, get up in the morning with your child and find opportunities to let them express themselves, and make choices within the guidelines that you've established as acceptable. This doesn't mean you can't say, "No," but you're deepening the levels of trust between you and your child while guiding them in the right direction.

Trust vs. Safeguarding

Today's household environment is full of potential temptations for our children, whether it is video games, the internet, cable television, or the plethora of electronic gadgets kids have at their finger tips.

Some parents adopt the attitude that because they *trust* their child, there is no need to add parental controls, restrictions or locks on these devices. But, we're all susceptible to temptation, and children are no different. Instead of setting your child up for failure with easy access to unrestricted, unmonitored content, it's crucial that parents act like parents and safeguard their child from making these poor choices.

For example, imagine a child that has been left home alone to finish their homework. They know that Mom or Dad will be gone for an hour or so, leaving them plenty of time to surf the internet on their own, without them looking over their shoulder. They may still even have time to do their homework too, before the parent returns home. What would most ten year olds choose to do?

And it's not their fault—they're kids being kids. It's difficult for anyone to resist temptations if the right circumstances present themselves. We need to remember that this is not a matter of trust. You can trust your child, and still implement safeguards for them. Without safeguards, you'll be basically setting them up to fail.

Instead, set an appropriate level of trust. Let them demonstrate that they can be responsible and make good choices, in a specific set of circumstances. Once they've proven they can handle that, give them more leeway, earning more trust and responsibility.

School Is Not the Ultimate Authority

As parents, we strive to raise our children with the same beliefs and values as ourselves. Often, these beliefs are complemented by what is taught in school, through the curriculum, corresponding with your own personal opinions. However, there may also be times when you disagree with a theory, concept, or point of view presented by the school. This could be your stand on the evolution/creationism debate, views on spirituality, sexuality, science, and/or many other issues.

Regardless of your beliefs, it's important that as parents, you communicate your thoughts and viewpoints to your children. During one-on-one time with your child, take the opportunity to chat with them about how your ideas differ from what they're being taught in school.

Yet, it can be challenging for children to understand how to learn and accept what is being taught in school once you've voiced your disapproval.

Consider starting the conversation something like this: "I know these are things you need to learn for school and that's okay. But, just because they're teaching you this and you need to learn it for the test, doesn't mean you need to believe it 100%."

From there, you may want to begin discussing why and how your opinion differs from that of the school system, discussing why these issues are important to you. In fact, through discussion, you'll be demonstrating your respect for your children by explaining your beliefs instead of simply trying to dictate what they should think.

Remember, you are the parent, not the school. When your child is young, this is the time when you're helping to establish the morals and values that will stay with them throughout the rest of their life. As a parent, this is your job, your responsibility, so don't be pressured to let the school make these important decisions for you; speak up and raise your children to share the values and beliefs you hold.

Sharing Values

Of course, you can't just say you believe in something and then act contrary to that—you need to demonstrate your own values and be consistent with them. For example, if you claim to believe in what a certain church preaches, it's a good idea to be involved in those types of activities with your family; your beliefs should be supported through your actions.

For instance, by being involved in church activities, your children will have an opportunity to learn some of the ideas and beliefs that you may hold, and then adopt them, too.

Supervision Is Needed!

When children are young, they need supervision. It's not a matter of merely trusting your children; it's also a matter of their safety. Remember, they're not adults—they're children. For young kids, they need Mom and Dad around.

Often, it's the period of time after school when kids are most likely to be left alone. For youngsters in elementary school, they need to have older siblings or adults around at home, instead of becoming a "latch-key kid." It's not productive or healthy for these young children to be by themselves at home for hours; they need guidance and direction, as well as supervision.

This is not to say that children in fifth and sixth grade can't be home for an hour alone after school. However, if kids are sitting home alone for three or four hours waiting for Mom or Dad, what are they taking away from that arrangement? Instead of benefitting them, this sounds like a situation that is based on the parents' convenience.

On another level, if other people around your neighborhood know that young kids are routinely home alone, such as every day after school; you're creating a potential risk for predators.

Keeping Your Child Safe

While no parent likes to think about the dangers their children may encounter, unfortunately there are predators who seek out children every day.

As responsible parents, we all need to educate our children on what to do if something feels unsafe, or if something bad has happened. For example, if they're being bullied at school, they need to tell a teacher or an adult at school, and tell you when they get home. Or, if someone is hurt, your children need to get the attention of an adult they know right away.

But what if someone has touched them inappropriately? Or, what if they feel uncomfortable with what an adult is doing? Without a doubt—your children need to know they can come to you.

— Predators

Pedophiles often get involved in programs that focus on kids, as this is their primary interest. A good way to reduce the chance of your child falling prey to an opportunistic predator is to "check out" the adults whom they come in contact with, such as volunteer coaches and scout leaders. For instance, find out if they have been through a fingerprint background check.

Certainly, I'm not suggesting that all volunteers who work with children are predators—the vast majority are genuine and sincere volunteers who dedicate their time, but as parents we need to stop trusting strangers just because they are adults and they seem "nice." In the interests of your child, become more cautious and investigate before you put them in a vulnerable position.

For example, a parent might assume it's okay for their child to go to the soccer coach's house for extra practice. But, if the parent hasn't been there before, themselves, then the child should not be going without your supervision. This is simply not okay; and your child needs to know that going over to an adult's house without first talking to you, even if it's their coach or team leader, is not okay.

Furthermore, the internet is also filled with predators, looking to prey on your children. For instance, chat rooms may include pedophiles posing as teens, hoping to connect with your kids. Educate your children—they shouldn't be allowed to chat with anyone they don't know.

> ### ~ A pedophile's home
>
> *Imagine a house filled with the latest toys—it may be a big screen TV, the newest video game console, the latest films, exclusive sports memorabilia, with pizza being eaten all the time. At first glance, most kids would love it! This is the bait ... and your child is the target.*

— Cause for concern

Situations with predators can often start quite "innocently." The adult may invite a child over to watch some sports clips, offer to help with homework, or even suggest extra help with an activity or skill. Then, when the child initially visits, the youngster is impressed by the adult's cool toys and fun environment, making them more willing to return.

Along the way, the predator may offer the child an alcoholic beverage, which many will happily try, despite knowing that they're too young to be drinking. However, at some point the relationship will change; and, when the child realizes what has happened, the pedophile may try to use the underage drinking to blackmail them for their silence. A typical youngster will think that they will certainly be in trouble for this poor choice, and many feel that their parents will never believe them and decide that they are at fault.

Of course, as adults we would recognize how the child was being manipulated and victimized; yet, we need to teach our children to come to us, no matter what the situation. As parents, we need to stress to our kids that they can tell us anything, that we'll be supportive and believe them, no matter what.

— Preventative tactics

Children who are lacking attention from Mom and Dad at home are often more susceptible to the advances of a predator. If children aren't getting enough attention at home, they will likely be more willing to receive it from another source. So, if they get that one-on-one time with Mom or with Dad, they'll be less inclined to seek it elsewhere—even from potential predators.

Overall, education is one of the best preventative techniques. Teach your children what to look out for in an age-appropriate way. They don't need to hear scary details, but simply: if they feel uncomfortable, unsafe, or if someone is touching them in an inappropriate way, they need to leave right away and tell you what happened. This approach is considerably more effective if you and your child have open lines of communication, as discussed earlier. That way, they'll feel comfortable coming to you and sharing what is happening early on.

Of course, by maintaining a two-way street of communication, you're creating a lifelong connection for sharing problems, as well as goals, values, and lessons in these formative years.

6 The Teenage Years

It's inevitable—your child is going to grow up. Perhaps they are already in their teens, maybe they're just around the corner, or you're anxious about these dreaded years to come. However, armed with insight and information, this notorious period need not be as dramatic as all the hype would lead you to believe.

Of course, as your child matures and develops, your relationship together will change and evolve alongside. Yet, instead of these years being filled with power struggles, it is possible to balance their yearning for independence and individuality with solid parental guidance and support.

Pick Your Battles

First and foremost—you need to decide which issues are worth fighting for. As parents, there may be many things our teens say and do that we disagree with. But we can't criticize, correct, or discipline every questionable action or choice. If you take a stand on every single issue, your teen will soon regard you as a nagging parent and pay little attention to your remarks, even when a serious matter comes along.

The parent becomes like a tired scent; initially, a smell can be strong and powerful, but if you stay in the room for a while, your nose will eventually get accustomed and not recognize the scent. So, while nagging may work initially, soon after nit-picking every little issue your teen will begin to tune you out. Ultimately, as parents, we need to pick which problems are most important and handle those head on.

Space, Boundaries, and Privacy

Teenagers are often noted for their messiness: not picking up after themselves, not keeping things tidy, and just being lazy around the house.

Consider the typical messy teenage bedroom—clothes, books, electronics, papers, and "stuff" simply everywhere. It's clear where they get their "untidy" reputation from. Furthermore, if this "style" of housekeeping doesn't match your own, this bedroom could be a zone for regular arguments between teens and their parents. "Make your bed," "Tidy up your room," "This is a pig sty in here!" repeat many parents, time and time again.

But, as your kids get older, it is important that they feel like they have their own space where they have a little freedom to be messy and just let loose. Therefore, it makes sense to loosen the rules on their bedroom, while maintaining clear expectations for the rest of the house.

For example, a family rule might be: it's not okay to leave dirty clothes on the living room floor, but if they don't smell, you can leave them on your bedroom floor. The teen is more likely to respect the first rule, knowing that those behaviors are tolerated in their bedroom.

But, this doesn't mean that the teenage bedroom is a rules-free zone. Parents need to establish boundaries, guidelines, and rules for this area. However, try offering your teenager some flexibility on the usual household rules. For instance, your teen is allowed to have snacks in their room, but needs to make sure they clean up after themselves. So, if the parent notices a "food-gone-bad" odor coming from the teen's bedroom, that's not okay.

It's about letting your child feel like they have their own space, but within a set of guidelines. This may take a bit of work on both sides. Like, if your teen decides not to make their bed, you shouldn't run in there and make it for them. If it's not to your liking, they can keep the door closed. There are many battles worth fighting—this isn't one of them.

To help both you and your teen be successful with this, discuss your expectations with them and the consequences if there are problems. By using logical consequences that are known up front, there will be no need to nag your teen over and over, because they'll know exactly what the consequence will be if they make a poor decision. This way, there doesn't have to be a major conflict and, as parents, you're not making any snap judgments out of anger.

Privacy is also a significant issue with teenagers. They have their space and want a certain amount of privacy. And, unless your child has given you reason to distrust them (like coming home smelling of marijuana or alcohol), you should respect them enough to allow some private aspects to their life.

Of course, if they do give you reason to think something suspicious is going on, then explain to them that you need to check things out with greater supervision because they've demonstrated this questionable behavior. Don't be surprised if they disagree with your assessment.

"For the Fourth Time!"

It can happen to any parent—you find yourself having to repeat everything three, four, or five times before your teenager finally listens to you. But if this is happening regularly in your household, let's look at what you're really communicating.

Here's what's happening. By repeating yourself time and time again, you're giving your teen the message that they don't need to listen to you until the fourth or fifth time. Basically, the underlying message you've given them is, "I need to say it five times, before I *mean* it." And, through your actions you've told them that they don't need to do anything, or respond until they hear it the fifth time.

Your teen has realized that nothing will happen if they ignore the first four times; there's no consequence for them. But, they've noticed that after the fifth time, Mom will get upset and they'll have to do the chore or action they're being told to do.

So, to break the cycle—let your child know what the expectations are, what the rules are, and then consistently follow through with them. For example, if your expectation is that they listen to you the first time you ask them to do something, ask them only once to take out the garbage. If they choose not to, then follow up with the appropriate consequence.

What an Embarrassment!

Many parents worry not only for the well-being of their adolescent, but also for themselves—what if my teen starts acting out, being dramatic, or being "gross" in public? What if they do something really embarrassing?

Is this a legitimate concern? Perhaps, as teens can be irresponsible, unpleasant, and insensitive. However, it is unlikely that parents will see "new" behaviors in a public setting; most teens have been exhibiting similar behaviors at home, often for quite some time, before sharing them in public.

The key is to deal with negative behaviors, mannerisms, or poor choices while your teen is displaying them at home. Address the issues and problems head on—have both parents get involved (and be on the same page), communicate clear expectations, and be consistent.

If you choose to ignore it, your teen may simply continue the embarrassing behavior, in private and public.

Striving for Independence

Part of being a teenager is seeking independence, but they still need boundaries and consistent consequences. They may not ask for them, or even like them, yet rules and boundaries create a sense of security and opportunity for growth.

As I've mentioned, children—no matter what their age—need to know what the rules are, what your expectations are, and what the consequences are, should there be problems down the road. With teenagers especially, talk about why these are the expectations and rules. This is a great opportunity to communicate with your child and help them make good choices throughout their teen years. They'll know what's acceptable and what isn't, they'll recognize an unsafe situation and know when to leave.

For example, if a friend invites them to a party with underage drinking, they'll recognize that Mom and Dad would not approve, and that maybe this isn't the best choice for them. While they're still making their own independent decision, you've guided them with your point of view, helping them choose the best course of action.

Rules and Expectations

With every age group, the key is to plan ahead and think before you react, no matter what has happened. With teenagers who tend to push the envelope and cross the line, it can be easy to overreact. However, if you "ground" them for thirty days, or take away all their privileges for two months, then you're left with few tools to help you effectively discipline your teen for the weeks or months ahead.

Instead, create a plan with your teenager, discussing your expectations and clearly defining the consequences; this eliminates the need for you to scream and yell, and lets your teen know what their choices are.

Using logical consequences, you'll help your teenager prepare for their future responsibilities in the outside world. You can help them understand that these consequences are the same as the consequences they'll see in the working world. For instance, if their boss at the fast food restaurant tells them to sweep the floor, and they don't, there will be consequences. By explaining and establishing rules and consequences at home, you're teaching them responsibility, accountability, and respect.

— Involving both sides in the discussion

Now that your child is older, it's important to get them involved as you discuss the expectations you have for your teen and appropriate consequences for negative behavior, as well as suitable rewards for positive behavior.

Of course, this conversation is best done when you're not in the middle of a conflict or disagreement, but instead when things are going well. And, if there are two parents at home, both parents need to be involved. So, ask for the teen's opinions generally, or find out their thoughts on specific issues.

For example, try sharing with your son or daughter some of your general expectations. Then, ask them what their expectations are.

Another starting point is to share your rules with your teen, and then ask for their input specifically regarding consequences. If your teen chooses not to mow the lawn, what do they think would be a fitting consequence? And if you're in agreement with their idea, great! If not, share with them your thoughts on a suitable consequence.

Parents ultimately have the final say, but respect your children enough to hear their point of view. You're not giving up your control or authority by simply hearing their opinions and listening to their thoughts and feelings.

By doing this, you're demonstrating that you value their input. And when consequences happen, your teen will be more likely to accept the outcome, because they were involved in the process. Overall, this helps create an environment where your teenager can deal with their consequences, without "hating you" for disciplining them.

~ No "secret" deals

Picture this: *Dad catches his son coming back home after sneaking out for the night. He chats to his son about his adventures and says, "Don't worry, I won't tell your mother about breaking your curfew. It'll be our secret."*

This kind of secret deal between parent and teen doesn't help either side. While the parent may want to protect the child, it's sending a mixed message—what is acceptable for one parent is different from what is acceptable for the other.

This is inconsistent discipline and doesn't help your child obey and respect your rules. Furthermore, it tends to cause problems with the other parent, as you've broken your deal with them, too. It doesn't mean you can't give them a break though if there were genuine extenuating circumstances.

— Mistakes are part of the learning process

No one wants their kids to learn a lesson the hard way. But, even after you've explained things to your child and talked about the possible consequences, for most children, they will still go ahead and make a really poor decision at some point.

As parents, we want our kids to learn from our mistakes. Yet the reality is some teenagers will need to learn the hard way. Mistakes will be made, but remember these are all part of the growing up process. While one teenager will listen to their parents' advice, another may not believe it and try their luck.

You may find this frustrating, because you've warned your teen, and have even been through it yourself—why won't they listen to you? Think back for a minute. How many times did your parents tell you not to do something, but you did it anyway? Sometimes we still do it, even if we know better.

You Don't Own Your Children

Though very few parents come out and say that they "own" their children, many parents, especially with young children at home, feel a sense of ownership over their kids. As they grow up, and are given more freedom and begin to express their own opinions, we as parents realize that we only have them for a short amount of time. Soon, they'll be on their own, leaving the nest.

In fact, the majority of the time that you'll know your kids, they won't be children, but adults. For that reason, it's important to work towards building a relationship based on respect instead of ownership or obligation. Take the time now, when you can, when they're young, to establish this mutual respect. If successful, instead of your teenager itching to get out of your home, saying, "I can't wait to leave because my Dad is such a jerk," they might enjoy their time in your home and benefit from their relationship with you.

Hugs

Showing affection to your children when they're teenagers tends to become more difficult. They're not interested in a hug, and might even pretend to be "too cool" for one. Long gone are the days when they used to rush home from school and couldn't wait to give you a big hug. They needed it then, and so did you.

People feel a sense of security from these displays of affection, both adults and children alike. Of course, we need more of this the younger we are, and by the time your child is a teenager, they can do without a hug most of the time. They may even say, "I'm not a kid, I don't need a hug anymore."

But that doesn't mean that you can't ask them for a hug, just for you. Though it may sound cheesy, I've said to my own children, "This hug is not just for you, it's for me too." Sometimes, that makes it okay. Your teenager will be able to handle that Mom or Dad might need a hug, and be able to give that. And as parents, we still enjoy a hug—after all, they're always going to be our kids.

The fact is that there will still be times when your teen will need a hug themselves. At this stage in their life however, it can be difficult to ask, so we can always tell them a hug is for us.

Give Your Teen a Way Out

Teens usually know what's right and what's wrong, a good decision versus a bad decision; although, when amongst friends or trying to impress others, following the right path can still be a challenge.

For example, a teen girl has heard about a party tonight and is invited to go. She knows it's not okay and that it won't be a good situation, but doesn't want to appear "uncool."

Instead of putting her in a difficult situation, let's give her a way out. She can simply blame her parents. "I wish I could go tonight, but I know my parents won't let me. Sorry, I can't do it."

This way, the teen can let her parents be the "bad guys" so she doesn't have to bow to peer pressure, giving her a way out of the situation without worrying about being pressured into it, or being teased for saying no.

By letting your child blame you, you're supporting them and encouraging them to follow the values and morals you've discussed as a family, and therefore staying true to themselves.

The Importance of Socializing

Socializing is an essential part of being a teenager. Teens should be socializing with other teens and be involved in sociable activities—whether it be school clubs, church groups, after-school sports, or any extra-curricular activity. They need this socialization and time with their peers, in addition to being involved with family activities.

But what about the child who sits in their room alone and is withdrawn from others; the one who has isolated themselves? This is a major red flag—something is going on. Talk to your teen and find out what they're dealing with, and what they're spending their free time doing.

Chances are, if they come home from school and go straight to their room, never leaving until they get ready for bed, there's a situation brewing that needs to be dealt with.

It could be a number of issues, such as being involved in activities that they shouldn't be involved in, or they could be immersed in a fantasy life, not based in reality, which is not going to be beneficial to them.

Teens need to have friends, and building friendships is an important part of growing up. These relationships help develop their peer interaction skills, as well as fine-tune their social skills; both of which are needed to find success later in life. Yet, if parents are not able to have an impact on this behavior, they need to seek outside help.

Online Communities

With a range of social networks to pick from, your teen might think their online friends are enough. But, if this is all they have, it's simply not the case.

Teenagers need to practice interacting with others in the real world. They need face-to-face contact; they need to be able to walk up to somebody and start a conversation. These teen years are about growth, which can include socializing with friends, being active in the community, doing activities like going to the beach or trying out skiing, or whatever their interests are.

Encouraging this involvement is much easier if it has been an established expectation for your children from a young age. This way, when they're teenagers, it's simply a continuation of these past activities. Otherwise, if they haven't participated in anything in years, it can be difficult to change when they're teenagers.

> ### ~ Extremes
>
> If a situation with your teenager becomes too much for you to handle, or you simply don't know how to help them, it may be time to get professional help. (We'll talk about this in the following chapter.)

Sexting

Never heard of the term "sexting"? You can be sure your teenager has. It means sending sexually suggestive text messages and photos, usually via cell phone, and its popularity is shocking.

In fact, a recent nationwide survey conducted by the National Campaign to Support Teen and Unplanned Pregnancy found that 20% of teenagers (thirteen to nineteen years old) had sent sexually suggestive photos of themselves at least once to others. That's one in five teenagers!

Consider a classroom full of thirty teens; of the fifteen girls in the class, chances are three of those have sent sexually explicit photos of themselves— remember these are thirteen-, fourteen-, fifteen-year-old kids!

The study also found that roughly 30% of teens have seen or received sexually explicit photos originally meant for someone else. So, a girl sends a suggestive photo to her boyfriend, and thinking it's pretty cool, he shares it with his friends.

These teens might think they are sending a "sexy" photo to a boyfriend or girlfriend, but that is rarely where the story ends. These photos are shared in locker rooms and even uploaded to the internet.

This humiliation can seem like the end of the world to a teenager. So, we need to be aware of what's going on in our teenager's life in order to help them deal with the situations they're facing. While it may be an awkward topic, or an uncomfortable conversation, as parents, we need to prepare our children for what they may encounter, experience, and see in their day-to-day lives.

Otherwise, you run the risk of your child thinking this is normal behavior and an acceptable way to interact with others. After all, with statistics such as one in three kids will be on the receiving end of a "sext," there's a good probability that your teen will experience sexting on some level.

— The *real* consequences of sexting

With such high popularity and awareness, sexting may appear normal or cool to teens. Yet, as parents we need to help them understand the possible long-term consequences of this type of action.

Sexting is not the same as sending a letter, where someone reads it and then throws it away; instead with today's technology, once something is sent electronically, it's out there forever. And, within thirty seconds, the photo that your daughter thought she sent to her boyfriend has been forwarded on, is now posted somewhere on a website, and viewed around the world.

Teenagers who send these photos may think it's all very innocent, just a little fun, but ask them how they would feel if their photo was still around twenty years from now! What if their own children could find it online? What if it hurts their chances of getting their dream job?

In fact, it's quite common today for employers to check out a job candidate's *MySpace* or *Facebook* page, as it tends to reveal a more authentic picture of the person they are hiring. Furthermore, if someone else has posted your sexy photos online, it's not always easy to remove.

Of course, these consequences are not a certainty, but as parents, we need to help our children understand that these types of choices *may* stay with them, possibly for their entire life. They can affect how other people perceive them and the judgments they make about their character.

Clothing Trends

Most teenagers use clothing to help express their individuality. It's one of the few areas where they have significant and regular autonomy. Whether it's an old shirt off the floor, an outfit to help them "fit it" with peers, or something coordinated top to bottom plus accessories to help them stand out from the crowd; clothing helps define our teens.

It's easy to simply let your child wear what they'd like. "It's just clothing," is the belief of many parents. While it does appear quite innocent, clothing often offers peers and parents clues as to the group a teen is associated with. Although it may not begin with those intentions in mind, your teen will likely be drawn into a group of peers who look and dress in a similar way. They'll assume your teen is just like them.

For instance, if your teen starts wearing white t-shirts, really long and baggy shorts, and high white socks, it's possible that they're involved in a gang. Or, if they start painting their fingernails black and dressing all in black, they may be part of the "goth" group.

As parents, even though we allow our teens the freedom and flexibility to choose what they wear, it's important that we still talk about these choices and create boundaries as to what are appropriate and inappropriate choices.

— Side-effects from a color choice

The issue with clothing isn't always the clothing itself; it's the associations that are implied or likely to be made because of it. For instance, if your child innocently thinks, "Oh, that looks cool, I'm going to try and dress like that tomorrow," that's fine. But when they begin to dress a certain way repeatedly, teens start connecting with others who dress that way.

The problem is that certain groups of teens have behaviors, beliefs, and values that may not be a positive influence. Some groups may not value education; they may encourage promiscuity or even promote substance abuse. If your teen becomes friends with these peers, they're more likely to follow a similar path.

Of course, there are always exceptions, but if your teen hangs out with peers who value education and talk about long-term goals, they're more likely to follow this road to success.

So, a teen that's on the right track—doing well in school and at home—can suddenly be drawn into a new group of friends with little in common, simply because they start dressing a certain way.

Insecure teens may feel safer with this group around them, even if they're not a positive influence. What we need to do as parents is pay attention when we start seeing changes in our teens. If they start to change their wardrobe and dress in a different way, speak up and ask them what's going on. The longer you wait, the more difficult it will be to effect change as they become more entrenched in the group.

— Step in, become informed

If you're worried that your teen may fall into a negative group or gang, but you're not sure what signs to look for, I recommend contacting their high school. Talk to the principal, vice-principals, or counselors and ask, "What kinds of clothing should I be aware of?" The school knows what the local gang attire looks like and other groups that may have negative tendencies.

Again, don't be concerned if your child wants to express their individuality with their clothing and hair styles, but turning a blind eye to what they're wearing and assuming there are no consequences is a naive approach.

As with most things, these issues are much easier to deal with in the beginning. If your teen starts adopting some of the group's values and becomes friends with them, it will be a lot more difficult to change and stop.

If you're concerned, sit down with your teen and talk to them. For example, try saying, "You have some options as far as how you dress, and there's a certain amount of flexibility, but it's not okay to dress like this," and explain your concerns. "I know a lot of people who dress like this are into things that are inconsistent with what we believe, and I'm not comfortable with this."

This issue can also be dealt with preemptively. Talk to your child when they're younger about the importance of education, setting long-term goals, family values and morals, including sexual behavior, drugs, alcohol, and gang affiliations. Your teen will be better equipped to make the appropriate choices in friends and feel more comfortable associating with peers who share similar beliefs. Ultimately, you'll be helping them stay on a more successful path into adulthood.

Change is a Red Flag

In addition to changes in clothing, if you see any *significant* changes in your teenager, pay attention—these can be red flags. For example, it could be changes to their eating habits or sleeping habits, or changes in their academic performance. Most often, this means that something is going on in your teen's life that you need to know about.

This is the time to communicate with your child. Talk to them, but also, don't be afraid to communicate with their school and teachers. Just like dealing with changes in clothing, issues are always easier to handle at the beginning; usually parents can have a significant influence on their teen and turn things around. Later on, however, once the problem has progressed, that is not always the case.

> ### ~ *Did you know?*
> Sexual promiscuity and gang affiliations are *not* uncommon for junior high (middle school) students.

Academics & Temptations

School is a significant part of your teenager's life; although instead of focusing on the academic side, many prefer working on their social standing instead.

As parents, it's important to explain to our children that even though they'll be presented with many fun alternatives to studying, such as parties, drinking, and girls/boys, high school academics will play a big part in shaping the rest of their life and career.

It's about long-term versus short-term gratification. We can all think of those popular kids in school who never studied, always partied, and always had an attractive boy or girl by their side. What people rarely see are the poor grades they get in school, and that for many, high school is the high point in their life. For this short-term gratification, they've sacrificed post-secondary education, and usually as a result, many of their future career choices. Frustrated and washed-up, these partiers are still sitting around with beer bellies in front of their apartment, with the same old, broken-down car, trying to relive their glory days when they're twenty-five, or even thirty-five.

This is not the future anybody really wants, so talk to your teen about the idea of delayed gratification. If they put forth the effort in their academics now, they'll have a greater opportunity to go to college; they'll be keeping the doors open on a wider range of career opportunities.

Additionally, by working hard in school now, they'll be setting up their future, so that one day they can support their own family and have their own home. By taking academics seriously now, they'll be investing in themselves, in their future. They will reap the rewards for the next sixty years.

On a personal note, I encouraged my children to participate in honors classes in junior high and high school. Very often the work was not any more difficult, but their classmates were generally more interested in academics.

Girlfriends/Boyfriends

Naturally, it's not easy to stay focused on studying when hormones are raging. There can be a lot of temptation—it's normal for teens to seek the attention of the opposite sex and be interested in having a girlfriend or boyfriend.

In fact, many teens who are studious may feel like they need to change themselves to attract the girl or boy of their dreams. Why bother trying hard at school when the girls are only interested in the "bad boys"?

Talk to your teen and explain that down the road, what they're doing now, academically, will be an asset. So the bad boys might be popular right now, but that won't be the case in a year or two. At college, there will be people with the same kinds of life goals—the character of people will change for the better. Also, they need to hear that high school is just a small part of their life and will actually be over quite quickly. So have fun, be involved, and enjoy the experience; just keep in mind that some of the choices they make will impact them for the rest of their lives.

Remember, you may have this chat with your teenager, and then have to have it again a week later. It can be very difficult for them, so as a parent— be supportive, sympathetic, and listen to them. This doesn't mean they can't be popular and have friends; they simply need to balance their academics with their social life.

> ### ~ Promiscuous girls
>
> Girls who are promiscuous often have low self-esteem. They may have been sexually abused, and this is the only way they know how to express love. They may also think, "I'm not worth much, so if somebody wants to use me, it's not a big deal." Many of these girls look for love anywhere they can, because they're not being supported, encouraged, or nurtured at home.

The P word—Pornography

Primarily an issue affecting boys, you must do what's necessary to protect your teenager from watching pornography. Dad may think there's nothing wrong with it, but at this young age, it opens doors prematurely that these children are not ready to deal with, often leading to problems down the road.

In fact, very seldom will you find a child or teen who is involved in criminal behavior, or any type of inappropriate sexual behavior who wasn't previously exposed to pornography. Porn changes and influences the way a young teen views the world around him. To begin with, it objectifies women; young men start to look at girls as objects, people without feelings or families, and simply as a tool to satisfy their sexual desires when they feel aroused. For a teenager who is exposed to pornography, this is the way they begin to look at girls—*how can I get them to satisfy me?*

Furthermore, whereas adults may use pornography for "personal pleasure," many teenage boys will want to experience the excitement in real life. Adults realize that pornography is false, but this fact is often lost on teens who don't have the same restraint and understanding as adults. The exposure to pornography can encourage teenage boys to become more sexually active, increasing their risks of teen pregnancy and sexually transmitted diseases.

If that isn't enough of a reason to stop your teen from viewing pornography, consider how they'll view the real women in their lives. Most women can't live up to the ones these teens watch in porn videos; after all, they're professionals who often have a lot of surgeries to help them look so perfect. But your teen's expectations will still be unrealistic—they'll be expecting a perfect ten and an incredible bedroom performance. If their girlfriend doesn't perform or look as good as those onscreen, they may find it quite easy to move on to the next relationship, leading to an unfulfilling, unsatisfied, and maladjusted sex life.

~ Self-fulfilling prophecy

Frustrated with your teen? Watch what you say. Kids who are told repeatedly: "You're a loser," or "You're never going to amount to anything," often end up fulfilling this prophecy. Teens who are told that they can't do anything right and will always fail, usually stop trying to succeed.

Instead, be positive and encouraging. Believe in your child and let them know it. "I know you can do it," or "I'm proud of you for trying your best," are much better alternatives.

A Rite of Passage—From Child to Adulthood

Teenage years can be the most challenging, formative, and confusing periods in a person's life. With so many forks in the road and decisions to make, teenagers—whether they like it or not—will ultimately appreciate having a parent around to guide them in making smarter choices. It won't be easy (for either of you) but in the long run, the effort will be well worth it.

7 Issues

Every day, our children will encounter new experiences and situations. While some of these new situations will be positive, others will not be so straightforward. The course of how to navigate your child towards the best route possible may not always be clear. Over the years, especially as a child becomes a teenager, odds are that, as parents, we'll be faced with some difficult issues and situations involving our kids that require serious attention, thought and action. Some parents will face minor issues, others perhaps more significant ones.

However, if we're more aware of the issues and able to recognize some of the symptoms, we'll be in the best position possible to help our kids. The first step is identifying the warning signs or red flags that we need to look for. What are they? And what does a parent do if they suspect their child is in trouble? At what point do parents need to get professional help for their child?

In this chapter, we'll look at some of the most prevalent issues facing our children today, and discuss some of the key warning signs and coping strategies that all parents need to be aware of.

Nature vs. Nurture

It's the timeless debate—when a child is born, is their personality and/or morality set in stone, or does a child's parents and environment nurture, shape, influence, and determine their character?

While many people used to believe that a child was born a certain way, and there was nothing that could be done to affect the outcome, today, many people consider that environmental factors can turn a child into a positive or negative member of society.

In my opinion, having counseled children and their parents for many years, it's a little of both theories; both nature and nurture play a role in how our children turn out.

For example, consider a pair of identical twins, who by nature are the same. Yet, if they are placed in two different environments, one twin may thrive and be successful, while the other may struggle. Obviously, that makes a strong argument for the importance of a nurturing environment. On the other hand, consider two children who live in the same environment, yet one of them is successful, while the other simply flounders. Does this not make a case for the nature argument, that these children were born with certain predetermined potentials or abilities?

Clearly, as parents we should recognize that each one of our children is naturally unique and different from the other. Strategies and techniques that will work for one may not work for the other. There's little we can do to impact the "blueprint" nature has given them. However, it's our job to help, encourage, and support them as they tackle the challenges life throws at them along the way. We can have a big impact on the environment they're raised in and the nurturing atmosphere that surrounds their upbringing. So, it's our responsibility to help them make the best choices, reach their potential, accomplish their goals, and become the best person they can be in all aspects of their life.

Denial

> **denial:** (noun)
>
> 1. a refusal to agree or comply with a statement; or
>
> a refusal to acknowledge
>
> 2. a psychological process by which painful truths are not admitted into an individual's consciousness
>
> ~*Collins English Dictionary*

Most parents would consider themselves relatively in tune with what's going on in their families. So, why then, when some parents see something amiss, do they seem to ignore the issue and do nothing? Simply put—they're in denial, whether it's out of fear, anxiety, or discomfort. But ignoring the problem, instead of addressing it head on, will not solve the crisis.

In almost all cases, there are warning signs that something has changed, something is not as it should be, something is wrong. And, it's up to us to pay attention and recognize these symptoms and signs of a problem. If we don't, it's very likely that our children will continue down this troubled path; as a result, they'll likely end up having to endure additional challenges and consequences, than had we stepped up and addressed the issue before it got out of control.

Denial doesn't make things disappear. In fact, the longer the issue or problem lingers, the harder it will be for you and your child to solve and deal with it. It's like dirty dishes after supper. If you deal with them promptly, they're not too difficult to wash. However, if you try to ignore them, the longer you leave them, the more they fester and the harder it will be to scrape off the grease and grime. So, what could've been handled quickly and effectively on day one has become a major issue, which will require much more serious and widespread attention to fix.

Instead of saying, "My son would never do this," or "My daughter isn't like that," as parents we need to step up to the plate and deal with these issues head on.

Eating Disorders

This first issue is more common than most people think; eating disorders are a widespread problem facing our teenage girls and boys. Yes, boys too are affected by this challenging issue. Anorexia and bulimia are the two main types of eating disorders. They're often found in teens who have a distorted view of themselves and their bodies; they may see themselves as being "fat" or ugly.

— Anorexia

Anorexia is, in essence, self-starvation. Whether it's because of peer pressure to look skinny or to imitate the models in the magazines, people who suffer from anorexia starve themselves to reach their unrealistic and unhealthy goal of becoming as thin as possible.

Warning Signs: Teens may exhibit compulsive exercising, dieting despite being thin, fixation on body image. Also they may wear inappropriate layers of clothing, even on warm days, and dress in a way to show little to no skin. For example, on a hot summer day, instead of wearing a t-shirt and shorts, a teen suffering from anorexia may be wearing layers and layers of clothing, even sweaters, to cover up their body, hiding themselves from others.

First Steps: Anorexia is a serious issue. Open lines of communication with your child, and talk to them, but get professional help for your teen. This is not something you can fix on your own. Try contacting the school counselor or principal as well as your pediatrician or doctor, a psychiatrist or psychologist.

> ### ~ Note
> If your daughter has been sexually abused in the past, she's at a higher risk of having an eating disorder. For her, what she eats becomes the one area in her life she can control. Furthermore, this teenage girl may believe that by losing weight, she'll stop developing into a young woman and keep a child-like appearance. As a victim of sexual abuse, her hope may be that if she looks like a child, losing whatever "figure" she had, she'll be safer—no one will be interested in her, and therefore no harm will come to her again.

— Bulimia

Bulimia is an eating disorder characterized by binging and purging. For example, someone who suffers from bulimia will eat large to very large meals, and then make themselves throw it up.

Warning Signs: Oversized portions at mealtimes, and obvious signs of purging in the bathroom (odor, visual residue, etc). Additionally, look for poor dental health, such as weak tooth enamel or rotting teeth, fluctuation in weight, and going to the bathroom after every meal.

First Steps: This is another serious issue that needs to be handled by a professional. As the consequences of bulimia can be fatal (the constant purging affects the vitamin and mineral levels in the body, creating a potentially deadly imbalance), parents need to take this issue very seriously.

Depression

It's quite common that kids will feel down from time to time as they get older. Breaking up with a girlfriend/boyfriend, getting a poor grade in school, or trying to figure out the social scene in high school are all challenging issues to deal with. For your teenager, these issues are real and may be very emotional for them. So, ask how they're feeling and let them share their thoughts, emotions and frustrations with you—it's a great opportunity to use your communication skills, and for your child to work through what they're feeling. Remember, they may need to speak about the incident repeatedly, so be patient and supportive, and listen.

When speaking to your kids, some will tell you that they're feeling depressed, while others will show you with their symptoms that they're feeling low.

> *Warning Signs:* Kids may appear sad, distant and disinterested in activities. Look for changes to their sleeping and eating habits, as well as their mood and loss of energy. Sleeping habits may change dramatically: they might be sleeping much more, or having restless nights. Eating habits usually change and the teen may lose their appetite altogether.

> *First Steps:* Approach your child and try to communicate with them to see what's going on. If this doesn't work, consider getting outside, professional help.

Depression & Suicide

If a depressed child is thinking of harming themselves, or even ending their life, resist the temptation to say: "Snap out of it," or "You're fine." In these situations, you may not get a second chance to help your troubled child.

> *Warning signs:* They may talk about not wanting to live anymore or that life's not worth living; they believe it's hopeless. They may start giving away cherished possessions to friends. Also

look for signs of increased isolation and a complete lack of interest in regular activities.

Next level: If your child ever talks about a plan of how they would end their life—i.e.: "I'd take an overdose of pills," this is a big step above just talking about suicide. Your child has thought this through in detail and at length; this is a much more serious situation.

First Steps: If they mention not wanting to live anymore, and talk about a plan, seek professional help immediately. This is URGENT and could be a matter of life and death.

Self-Mutilation

While self-harming, cutting, or self-mutilation is not often discussed, the issue is actually fairly prevalent in our teenagers. Many might ask, "Why would anyone hurt themselves, repeatedly?" And if you ask a child who performs this type of self-harm, they themselves may not even know why they do it. However, those who do answer the question often say that it makes them feel better, and releases the pain they feel inside. This is because they often have low self-esteem or difficulty handling their emotions.

Self-mutilation is a coping method for kids who have trouble expressing themselves; these children may be depressed but simply can't articulate or work through what they're feeling.

Warning Signs: Cuts or burns on their skin. Or, teens who insist on covering up their bodies with clothing, even on warm days. If concerned, ask to look at their arms, a common location of evidence of self-harm.

First Steps: Talk to them about what's going on, and consider professional help if the issue persists.

Date Rape

While date rape does occur in high school, this issue is actually increasingly common in college settings. It's crucial that our children know that date rape is a real issue and needs to be reported if it happens to them.

And, while most colleges are prepared to deal with incidents of date rape, many girls still tend not to report it. They may feel responsible if they invited the boy back into their dorm room; they may even think that no one is going to believe them. These are normal feelings, but we need to educate our children on this issue, especially if they're heading away from home for the first time.

> *Preventative Tactics:* Explain to your daughter that if it does happen to her, she needs to report it because people will believe her. Also, reiterate to both sons and daughters that they can say "no" at any time. For example, you can invite your date back to your room, you can be "fooling around," and still you can say, "No, I don't want to do this." If your date continues to pursue and forces you to have sex, then it's date rape. Having your teen daughter take a self-defense class is also a good idea.

Sexually Transmitted Diseases

STDs are preventable. Teens need to be aware of the risks when having unprotected sex. With this issue, consider what your values are as parents and as a family. Society may support the idea of teens being sexually active, and if you agree, that's fine. But if you don't—let your teen know your thoughts and beliefs on this subject.

Of course, these are viewpoints that you should be sharing and discussing when they're young; if you wait to talk about sex until your child is sixteen, chances are they might already be sexually active. If you start sharing your values and talking openly to your children about all issues, including sex and STDs, as they're growing up, then you will have the groundwork to re-discuss the topic when they're older, building on your past conversations. This is a much more advantageous position to be in, rather than suddenly bringing up sex and STDs out of the blue.

Does the idea of having a sex talk with your child make you uncomfortable?

Put your kids first and deal with your own discomfort later.

Furthermore, by openly discussing these issues with your teen, should they ever get an STD, they're more likely to come to you for help. As many STDs can be treated, let your child know they can come to you if something's wrong, or they're in pain. Then, you can ensure that whatever situation they're in, you'll be able to get them the treatment they need.

Preventative Tactics: It's not rocket science—explain to your teen that the best protection from STDs is abstinence. If they are going to become sexually active—use a condom to give the most protection against catching a disease from their partner. Finally, remind your teen that they can get a disease or become pregnant the first time and every time.

First Steps: Start the conversation about sex and STDs, in an age appropriate manner, before your child hits their teenage years. Share your thoughts and values with them, opening up an ongoing dialogue between you and your kids.

~ *Misconceptions*

When kids are misinformed, they make choices based on incorrect information. For example, many people believe that a girl can't get pregnant if the guy doesn't have an orgasm, or "pulls out" before ejaculation. This belief is false. Due to a small amount of seminal fluid (discharge)present *before* the guy has an orgasm, the girl can still get pregnant.

— Scare tactics

What if you find that despite being open and honest with your teenagers, they still seem to be eager to have sex and/or unprotected sex? Instead of making it a black and white issue, try adding some color with images. Sometimes by sharing with your teenager the specifics of an STD, such as herpes, it can help them to understand the serious repercussions that one poor decision can have.

For instance—there is no cure for herpes. While there are medications that help deal with the symptoms, once you get the disease, it will reoccur, coming and going, for the rest of your life. But just what is herpes? Try showing your teen photographs of an outbreak of genital herpes. Ask them, "*Can you imagine having blisters and sores in your genital area?*"

This usually makes teens quite uncomfortable and rightly so, as nobody wants to contract herpes. However, continue to explain to them that if they have unprotected sex with someone infected with herpes, there's a good chance the disease will be transmitted to them. Furthermore, this will mean that they'll be in a position to spread the disease to their sexual partners, including their spouse one day down the road.

Most kids will look at this information and take the warning to heart.

I met this girl last night....

Imagine the excitement of a young teenage boy who meets a girl on a night out, and that same night she's willing to have sex with him....

Sounds like a teenager's dream? Perhaps, but parents need to ensure their teens understand the whole picture. If this girl is willing to have sex with you, after having just met you, how many other guys was she willing to have sex with the first time she met them?

Along the same lines, talk to your teen about how having sex with one person is like having sex with every one of their past sexual partners, too. If any one of their partners had a disease, they may have passed it on, and now your partner is possibly passing their disease onto you. So, it's not just about being intimate with that one person; sometimes you're being intimate with numerous people, even dozens of strangers!

Drug & Alcohol Abuse

Substance abuse, be it drugs or alcohol, is a widespread societal issue. Though many of the warning signs are quite recognizable, if a parent is in denial, these issues and addictions can continue to develop and grow, further harming the affected teenager.

> *Preventative Tactics:* Stay aware and informed about your child's life. Communicate with them and find out how they're doing, and what they're doing with their time, also where they're going after school or on a Saturday night. If you're not getting enough answers from them, try contacting the school to see how their academics are going. You may find out they've been skipping third period for the last week, suggesting that something irregular is going on in their lives.

> *Warning Signs:* Key signs include major changes in their social circles, difficulty getting up in the morning, disappearance of money or objects being sold to buy drugs. As well, there may be significant changes in the way they dress and the hours they keep. For instance, they may be staying out much later than they used to.

First Steps: Again, communication is key. Talk to your teen. However, if this is an ongoing problem with signs of addiction, get professional help. Often there are free twelve-step programs available. Talk to a school counselor for resources.

— Selling drugs

While it could be thought of as the next step after drug use, selling drugs is also a separate, stand-alone issue. And, it goes without saying that this is not an appropriate way for your teenager to earn extra money—unless they want to go to jail.

Warning Signs: If you suddenly see your child with money, or clothing that they normally wouldn't have, ask where they're getting it from. The extra money from selling drugs can be substantial, so be aware of any significant and sudden changes in their financial habits, as these can be indicators that something's going on. There may also be increased phone usage at all hours of the day/night.

First Steps: Confront your teen and talk to them about the risks of illegal behavior and possible consequences for both them and the community around them. Seek outside help.

Dating

What age do you think your kids should start dating? Do they know your thoughts and beliefs? If not, talk to them about what you think is appropriate and at what age. This is a popular topic at school, and very often there's considerable pressure for kids to have boyfriends and girlfriends early on, even starting as young as eleven and twelve years old. Those choosing not to partner up may be teased or even ostracized by the group.

Without a girlfriend/boyfriend, the child may feel like a loser, or that something's wrong with them, but take the time to explain that this is certainly not the case. For example, point out to your young teen that for the majority of their life, they'll be in a relationship; there's only a small window when they won't be—these younger years.

This gives kids the chance to enjoy a sense of freedom and flexibility to go out with whomever they want, to stay home if they'd prefer, to hang out with friends, and generally to figure out their own ways through this period in their lives. Too often when dating, a teenager is compelled to do certain things, or only spend time with their boyfriend/girlfriend, because that is what is expected: "It's Friday night, of course we're going out together."

> *Preventative Tactics:* Explain the advantages to your child. Also, give them a "way out" with their peers. For instance, if the house rule is "no dating until sixteen" your teenager is now armed with the phrase, "My parents say I can't date until I'm sixteen." With this information, they're less likely to be bullied, teased or pressured as it's not their choice not to date, but yours.

Teen Pregnancy

Few girls have the goal of becoming pregnant as a teenager, although teen pregnancies are a fact of life. As parents, we need to talk frankly to our sons and daughters about the consequences of raising their own baby, with a clear picture of the risks and responsibilities involved, so they might make better, more informed choices regarding unprotected sex.

Some teens think that having a baby will be great, as they'll have a friend for life. However, we can help them understand it's not fun and games— it's a full-time job, with no time off. Everything will change—education, employment opportunities, their social life. This is something that can be avoided and should be saved until they are adults.

> *Preventative Tactics:* Create a Prevention Plan with your teen, to help them avoid being in a tough situation. For instance, if it's midnight and your teen is with their boyfriend/ girlfriend, in the bedroom alone, it may be difficult to say "no" to having sex, and easy to forget about the risk of pregnancy. However, if your teen makes that decision to say no earlier in the day, you can help them create a plan to avoid being in that situation.

> Brainstorm some alternative options, or ways to end the night. What are safer situations and environments for spending time with their boyfriend/girlfriend?

Peer Pressure

Peer pressure is a reality of your child's life. It increases as they get older and throughout their teenage years, with the pressure being applied to increasingly more serious issues also.

Talk with your kids about the fact that peer pressure exists and that people are going to encourage them and push them to do things. Remind your teen that if it's something they don't want to do, or is inconsistent with what your family believes, then they should say no and, if necessary, walk away from the situation.

Friends might pressure them to drink alcohol or use drugs, to be promiscuous, to cheat on a test, to steal, or even to harm someone else. No matter what your child is being pressured to do, they should try to take a step back and look at the situation for themselves, before acting.

> *Preventative Tactics:* Prepare your kids for peer pressure—they'll be in a position to handle it, if they're expecting it. Help them develop a prevention plan or a strategy ahead of time. For example, can they call you if they're at a party with no safe ride to take them home?

Abuse

Whether it's physical, verbal, sexual, or emotional abuse, none of these are acceptable, and consciously we must make choices to put an end to this cyclical problem. If it's happening in your family, stop denying the signs and symptoms and protect your children.

> *Physical Abuse:* As mentioned previously, punishment can quickly lead to the physical abuse of a child. As parents, we need to be aware that hitting our children is not acceptable. Remember, if a teacher sees a mark on a child at school, they're obligated to report it, immediately. Make smart, healthy choices, always with the best interest of your child first, when disciplining and giving your children consequences.

> *Verbal Abuse:* This refers to how we interact with our kids. If you're constantly condescending toward them, or continually putting them down, always yelling, calling them names—this is verbally abusive. This includes calling them stupid, dumb, or an idiot. Choose your words carefully, and take a cooling off period if you tend to speak abusively out of anger.

> *Sexual Abuse:* Seriously traumatizing, disturbing, and scarring, this type of abuse is clear-cut and needs to be addressed immediately.

Emotional Abuse: Going hand-in-hand with neglect, emotional abuse refers to the care or lack of care that we provide for our children. As parents, we need to ensure they have adequate supplies in terms of food, clothing, and the basic necessities. Neglecting these is considered abusive behavior.

— Sexual abuse—Long-term effects

For a girl who was sexually abused at an early age, there are issues that continue as she develops into a woman. Specifically, if the parents choose not to seek help for their daughter, very often the girl will have a difficult time expressing love throughout the rest of her life. Common symptoms include difficulty with intimacy in a marriage (due to negative feelings about sex), or increased promiscuity, as this is the only way she knows how to express love (resulting in numerous partners and/or spouses).

Therapy is almost always needed, and may also be helpful both when they're younger and once again when they become teenagers; this can be a challenging time as they suddenly start seeing things in a more sexual way, creating new issues with the past abuse. It is important to find a therapist that specializes in child abuse issues to help your teen.

Anger Management

We all get angry from time to time; however, some people genuinely have difficulty dealing with their emotions of frustration, irritation, teasing, or taunting. If your child shows signs of having anger management issues, it's important to help them work through their feelings and create some coping techniques that help them both socially and emotionally.

Warning Signs: A short temper, urges to physically fight with others, constant verbal altercations, an inability to work through their feelings.

First Steps: As this issue also commonly affects parents, specific strategies to help those affected with anger management issues are discussed in depth in the section on taking care of yourself.

Becoming Desensitized to Violence

Ongoing exposure to any stimuli can lead to desensitization. Whether it is due to the nagging of a parent or the constant pestering of a sibling, kids will also become desensitized, just like adults. Unfortunately, in addition to tuning out these typical household issues, many kids are now being exposed to images of violence to a level of normalization.

Video game producers will argue that this is not the case; however, in my experience, I've found that children who have had repeated exposure to violent imagery—be it through violent video games or graphic TV and film—become, in fact, accustomed to seeing these disturbing images.

As parents, do we want our children to see pictures of killing, hurting, rape, and torture at all, let alone repeatedly? While these would be shocking to a child the first time they saw it, if it was something they watched over and over, as in the case of a video game, they are bound to acclimatize to this style of imagery. This is the "nurture" aspect of nature vs. nurture.

It's important that we remember how these types of images affect our kids. For that reason, it's not okay to take young children—twelve, thirteen, and fourteen year olds—to R-rated movies filled with extensive violent scenes. Furthermore, parents shouldn't be buying mature rated video games for their young kids to play. What are they learning from a game that focuses on killing police officers, stealing cars and beating up prostitutes? Are these the images you want your children to become familiar with, so much so, in fact, that it doesn't affect them anymore?

> *Preventative Tactics:* Stop equating the TV, video game, and movie theater with a babysitter for your kids. Check what they're watching and make sure it's suitable and age-appropriate.

~ *Music Messages*

Much like imagery, if a child hears a certain phrase or concept repeatedly they'll also become desensitized to the words. While "pimp" and "hoe" are now commonplace lyrics, if a child idolizes singers who sing songs with these messages, this can lead to negative views that objectify women. Is this in their best interest? Will they not begin to see their relationships with a skewed view of reality? Be aware of what they're listening to and the messages they're absorbing along the way. Look for ratings on the CD.

Gangs

Kids need to feel a sense of belonging. If parents have created a nurturing home environment, children will likely feel like they belong and are part of your family. Yet, if parents are unavailable, it's natural for kids to seek this acknowledgment and attention elsewhere. In essence, this means that other people are going to raise your children. Gangs are usually available to fill this hole in their lives.

Sometimes a child can get brought into a gang environment quite innocently, too. If Mom or Dad isn't around, and their friends are playing outside, how many teens are going to sit indoors by themselves? Kids find ways to occupy their time, and if we're not there to influence their choices, someone else will be.

Which would you choose? An hour of overtime or an extra hour with your kids? While the extra money might be attractive, spending an extra hour with your children will pay greater dividends in the long run. We need to view the time we put in with our children as valuable, even priceless.

> *Preventative Tactics:* Provide supervision for your child. It's very uncommon to have a teenager in a gang when you have been actively involved in their life. Know where your child is, who their friends are, and where they're going when they go out. This does not mean being a "helicopter parent"—someone who shows up and hangs out at school all day to watch their child—but taking an involved role in their life can be crucial. Instead of saying, "Be back by 9 p.m.," ask questions—who, what, where are they going?

> *Warning Signs:* Look for changes in clothing and hairstyles. Certain "looks" can suggest that someone associates with a specific group or gang. Also, watch for changes in academics, friends, and attitude; use of hand signs; graffiti on their possessions.

> *First Steps:* Take a greater interest in how your child is spending their free time. Become involved in their life and provide additional supervision as needed. Also, contact your local police department for information on gang prevention programs in your area.

Helping Your Child with a Tough Situation

While we've discussed specific strategies and techniques on how to address some of the more serious issues you may face as a parent, it's also vital for your children to understand these, too.

Generally speaking, teach your children how to say "no." Remind them that no matter where they find themselves, and at whatever age, they can and should tell an adult about what's going on if they're in trouble.

Education

Almost everyone would agree that a good education is one of the most valuable tools for a child's future. It goes without saying that graduating high school, and furthermore, post-secondary education, opens doors of opportunity for people, especially in regards to employment. I believe that a solid education will help in many other aspects of a child's life, as well.

Supporting this view, the American Human Development Project and the United Way jointly published a study in 2009, "Goals for the Common Good: Exploring the Impact of Education," which highlighted how the level of education a person has greatly impacts their life as a whole.

Consider these statistics:

- **Life expectancy:** On average, the more education people have, the longer they live.

  Those who acquire education beyond high school have an average life expectancy that is seven years longer than those whose education stops with high school.

- **Low birth-weight:** Infants born to less-educated mothers are more likely to have low birth-weight, which is associated with developmental delays and infant death.

- **Murder:** A one-year increase in the average level of schooling in a community is associated with a 30% decrease in the murder rate.

- **Obesity:** Obesity has increased among all Americans, yet the more educated are less likely to be overweight or obese.

- **Income:** The median annual earnings of Americans 25 and over who did not complete high school are less than \$18,500, while those who completed high school typically earn nearly \$26,000. College graduates earn \$44,000 annually, and those with graduate or professional degrees typically earn \$57,500.

- **Poverty:** Education is the single most important factor in the determination of a person's poverty status: almost 24% of the adult population without a high school diploma is poor, compared to 11% of those who are high school graduates and only 3.6% of college graduates.

- **Unemployment:** The less education a person has, the more likely he or she is to be unemployed. A high school dropout is four times more likely to be unemployed than a college graduate.

- **Voting:** In the 2004 presidential election, those with a college degree were 50% more likely to vote than high school graduates, and two and a half times more likely to vote than high school dropouts.

- **Incarceration:** Nearly three-quarters of state inmates did not complete high school; fewer than three percent completed college or more.[1]

When faced with these statistics, the importance of education becomes even more apparent. Think about it—by completing high school, your child is greatly improving their future outlook.

So, don't be afraid of sharing these facts and figures with your children—if they've been having a difficult time prioritizing academics, then talking to them about the long-term effects and rewards of an education may help—from the advantages of a higher income to the fact that they'll be able to support a family of their own one day.

Step-by-Step

With all of these possible issues to confront, the key is taking it one day at time and setting achievable, short-term goals together—step-by-step.

---

1   American Human Development Project and United Way. "Goals for the Common Good: Exploring the Impact of Education" http://www.liveunited. org/file/common_good_forecaster_full_report.pdf (accessed June 5, 2009)

For instance, if your son or daughter wants to drop out of school, don't focus on getting them to college. Instead, work with them and come up with a plan to make it through the day, attending all their classes. Then, set a goal for a week ahead. Once these short-term goals are consistently being met, together look a little further down the road.

This type of approach is especially helpful if your child (or you) is feeling overwhelmed; simply look at what needs to be done today and worry about that. Tomorrow you can work on tomorrow's issues.

~ Contact the School

If your child is having difficulty with their academics, reach out to their teacher. Depending on the challenges your child is facing, you may need the teacher's continued support to help your child get back on track. Ask them for the help *you* need: a daily progress report, a weekly update, a phone call when a test date is set. The teacher may forget and need to be reminded—remind them. If you explain the situation and the goals you've set together with your child, most teachers will help. And don't be embarrassed about asking them—your kids are more important than school politics.

Rebellion

It's natural for teens to struggle with issues as they travel the path towards independence. Usually this is characterized by the familiar "teenage rebellion" that is so often associated with this age group. This rebellious, authority-challenging phase is normal for teens—they're simply trying to break free and spread their wings. Let your kids know this is normal, but not an excuse for disrespectful behavior.

Consider the space shuttle, which uses over two million pounds of fuel in order to break away from Earth's gravitational pull, yet uses hardly any to fly around once in outer space.

Basically, as parents we may see more conflict, angst, tension, and issues in our household while our teenage is trying to "break free" from our family and achieve a certain amount of independence (which is good, because we want them to become independent, eventually). Of course, remember, they'll be using a huge amount of energy in the process, much like the space shuttle. Once your child has achieved this goal, things will simmer down and mellow out. The hostility will dissipate and a certain amount of stability will ideally return to your home.

With that in mind, give your teen the chance to begin spreading their wings, and be there for any issues that arise along the way. In the end, this will help ease their transition into this next phase of their life, and you will be there to assist them on their journey.

8 Role Modeling

Kids need role models; whether they look up to a famous athlete, music artist, or someone closer to home, our children will look for direction and acceptable behavioral cues from this person. Often, it will be someone they respect, someone who they believe is successful, yet it could also be someone who isn't the best role model to base their lives on.

Of course, as parents, we too will be role models for our children—for better or worse. Our daily interactions and approaches to life's challenges will shape the attitude, behavior, and choices of our kids. The level of involvement we have in their lives will determine just how much their behavior is influenced by ours.

Nurturing Our Children

As discussed in the previous chapter, nurturing is an important part of raising our kids. For instance, if we compare a child to a block of ice, each block will be unique and different, just like every child. However, instead of the chiseling tools used by a sculptor, as parents, it is our nurturing environment, parenting choices, and even personal choices, which shape and sculpt our children. Everything we do and share with them will help to determine the values, morals, ethics, and priorities in our child's future.

Nevertheless, while one parent may demonstrate positive choices and represent a good role model, another may exhibit questionable habits, poor decision-making, and actually be a negative role model. Yet, if we're aware of this—that our choices and actions may be mirrored by our children—we can think twice before acting, ensuring that we're setting the best possible example for our kids.

As the old saying goes: **the apple doesn't fall far from the tree**! As your child grows and develops, they will emulate you.

Kids May Look Elsewhere

While the parent should ideally be a role model for their child, if Mom or Dad isn't home, and appropriate kinds of modeling aren't available for their kids, the reality is that children will look elsewhere to find role models.

And, today's top role model picks are incredibly different from twenty or thirty years ago. Long gone are the days when children wanted to be firefighters or cowboys when they grew up. When I speak to young children and adolescents about future goals, many want to be a hip hop artist or a pro basketball or football player. With all the media coverage, financial earnings, and glamorous, high-profile lifestyles that these celebrities have, kids perceive this as the epitome of success. They look up to these people and aspire to be like them.

Though some of these artists and athletes lead exemplary lives, many others are simply not ideal role models for our children. And they don't have to be, that's not their responsibility, it's ours. But as parents we need to be aware of who our children idolize and model their behaviors after, so that we can discuss their choices and actions, and be sure our children are headed in the right direction.

For example, if a young boy respects and constantly listens to a rapper whose songs are womanizing in nature, or even derogatory to women, these beliefs and views may eventually resonate with him, too. If the hip hop artist is shown driving fancy cars, covered in "bling," with girls on each arm, are these really appropriate goals for a young boy to have?

In fact, I speak with many teens who tell me that they aspire to be a "pimp"! Of course, it's not always in the conventional use of the word, but instead of a monogamous relationship, these teens are hoping to surround themselves with multiple women, just like their idol.

Moreover, while a pro athlete on the surface is sending a better message:

one of perseverance, hard work, good health, etc; it has become more and more commonplace to see these sports stars in the news for scandalous reasons instead.

Regardless of whether or not our kids look up to these types of role models, as parents, we need to provide guidance towards the best course of action, and be role models ourselves. Without this support, children will follow another dominant voice in their life—which may be one of these questionable celebrity role models, peers at school, or a stranger you don't know about.

> *~ Who would you pick*
> *as the ideal role model for your child?*
>
> *For your daughter: the latest socialite, or a successful woman in the family?*
>
> *For your son: a notorious rap artist, or a hardworking father-figure?*

It Takes All Kinds

Certainly, it's important to keep in mind the many influences, interactions, and possible role models your child will encounter at school. It's easy to forget, but because almost everyone goes through the high school system, it's like a microcosm of the outside world. Your kids will meet the entire spectrum of future citizens in this high school environment. In any given high school, you will find future drug dealers, alcoholics, and criminals, as well as doctors, dentists, politicians, lawyers, and teachers.

For that reason, as role models will be found in school, within peer groups, we need to stay in the loop and be aware of who our children are socializing with, and what groups they're hanging out with. Talk to them about the path some of their peers are heading down. Even if they attend a "good" high school, with "nice" kids, it takes all kinds.

Generation after Generation

In most families, children observe and absorb what their parents are teaching them, on multiple levels. In many cases, this includes opinions about education, politics, social values, ethics and morals that they hear around the dinner table or in passing conversation.

Unfortunately, the same is true of those children born into less fortunate situations. For example, it's not uncommon to find someone who lives in poverty, on public assistance in an inner-city environment, whose parents and grandparents were in the same position. Generational cycles of poverty continue in part because people are repeating the behaviors they've learned at home without any hope or belief that things can change.

Many parents in an impoverished situation may feel helpless in helping their children break out of the cycle, but it is possible.

~ Picture this

A few years back, I was counseling a twelve-year-old girl. As I do with many youngsters, I asked her what her goals and ambitions are. Her answer: she wanted to have a baby as soon as possible. Why? She replied that if she had a baby she could get on welfare, receive monthly checks, and then she'd be "taken care of."

Clearly, she had heard this rationalization before and had learned this information at a young age. In essence, the choices, decisions, and comments that we model for our children can be determining factors in their future.

Breaking Free from the Cycle

Consider the history, success and achievements of Judge Sonia Sotomayor, the first Hispanic woman to be nominated to the U.S. Supreme Court: Born in the South Bronx (NY), she was raised by her mother, in the housing projects, after her father (who had only a third-grade education) tragically died when she was nine years old. Though living in what many would consider poverty, Sonia's mother, Celina, emphasized the importance and power of education and strong values, giving her two children the tools they needed to break free from this environment. Further emphasizing the power of knowledge, Celina even purchased encyclopedias for her children to read, despite working within a limited income.

Against all odds, both Sonia and her brother (now a physician) went on to lead successful lives, attending university, and earning post-graduate degrees. Sonia attended Princeton, and later Yale Law School.

Clearly, this was not taking the "easy road," but instead one of hard work and determination. This family could have so easily stayed in the projects and continued to live a life of poverty. Yet, Celina Sotomayor encouraged her children otherwise, by prioritizing and supporting their education.

Regardless of personal political opinions, the story of Judge Sotomayor is an incredible example of how a person can break free of this cycle of poverty.

Modeling Values—Monkey See, Monkey Do

Role modeling is one of the key ways we communicate our values and ethics to our children. This includes things like being kind, generous, assertive, and compassionate as well as our work ethic and perseverance. Essentially, we're role modeling appropriate behavior through our actions every day.

For example, Dad may say, "Don't yell at your mother," but if he yells at Mom all the time, that's the example he's truly showing his kids. Characteristics and behaviors like these are commonly passed on, generation to generation.

Even more subtle beliefs and behaviors can be mirrored by our children, too. For instance, if a parent has an issue that they're trying to deal with, it's typical for this problem to spill over and affect their child. "But my kid never saw me doing (BLANK)!" is the common reply. Nevertheless, their child is now exhibiting a similar behavior.

Basically, kids are observant and usually quite in tune with what's going on, whether you think you're doing a good job of hiding it or not. Always remember: Monkey See/Monkey Hear, Monkey Do.

Unconditional Love

An important concept to role model for your children is the idea of unconditional love. As parents we need to always show and tell our kids that we love them. By role modeling this behavior, we're teaching children that they can love someone unconditionally, but still be upset, hurt, or angered by their behavior. Your children will learn that you respect them and love them, no matter what.

Kids need to understand this, so that when they're being disciplined, or when they know they've done something wrong, they'll never question your love for them. They'll understand that while you may not approve of their choice or action, and there may be consequences, your love for them will not be swayed.

By modeling this type of love, you'll be teaching your child how to love their child one day.

Relationships

In addition to modeling unconditional love, it's important to recognize that we're also teaching our kids, through our words and our actions, how to be mothers/fathers and husbands/wives. How we behave and interact in relationship to others will serve as guidelines for our children in their current and future relationships.

Ultimately, it is through us that our children learn how to behave in society, how to treat their partner, their friends, and even themselves—all simply by observing you.

Some aspects of role modeling relationships may also be more subtly communicated, such as the right age to get married or start having sex. For example, when counseling couples who were married young, in the age range of seventeen to twenty, it often comes out that their parents were married young, too. I'm not saying people should or shouldn't be married at a young age; however, it's important to recognize that even these life choices, which might be decided long before we have kids, may still have an effect on them, all these years later.

Consider a young couple in love; they're both eighteen years old. In a household where the parents were married young, Mom and Dad might encourage the youngsters to tie the knot, just like they did. However, even if parents don't encourage them, the teens may still think it's okay because it worked out fine for their parents. By contrast, in a family where Mom and Dad finished college before getting married, it may be suggested that the teens wait a few more years as, "there's no rush to settle down." Ultimately, they will still make their own decision but it will be affected by their role models.

Your life experiences will naturally shape your views and, by consequence, the way you parent. However, it's important to keep in mind what's best for your child and guide them accordingly. Of course, if it was good enough for Mom or Dad, many kids will think it's good enough for them.

Separation & Divorce

There are times and situations where separation and/or divorce may be the right choice. In abusive and unhealthy relationships, it may even be the best choice. Although it's important to recognize that even in these types of situations, we're acting as a role model for our children.

For example, with so many marriages ending in divorce today, more and more children are seeing these types of family issues and changing dynamics. Will your children see you and your partner work to get through a rough patch? Will they see people problem solving together, actively trying to resolve any issues that arise? Or, will they see two people disconnected and disinterested in saving their marriage?

How you act will shape and influence how they will act in their future relationships. So, what message will you send your child through your choices and actions?

This is not to say that divorce shouldn't happen. However, it's just become so commonplace in today's society that many couples don't think twice about the repercussions of this decision and how they will handle the challenges before, during, and after a marital break-up.

Love—Not a Feeling, but a Decision

A common reason people get divorced is because they "fall out of love" with their partner. Nevertheless, I find that if love is viewed as a decision, rather than a feeling, it can help a married couple through a difficult time, instead of dwelling on the feeling of falling out of love.

Basically, feelings come and go—just like anger, happiness, frustration, sadness, feelings of love can also fluctuate. Imagine the feeling of love like a small boat on the ocean. If viewed from the shore, the small boat is bounced up and down with every little wave—those are our emotions.

However, if we view love as a decision, as in, "I've decided I'm going to love this person," then no matter what our emotions say or what we're feeling on a given day, not loving them isn't an option. This decision encourages you, as a couple, to make things work in your relationship. Obviously, there are exceptions, but in healthy relationships, this tends to make things easier.

With love being a decision, you don't have to feel excited about your partner every single day, but you can still love your partner. In this scenario, imagine love being a big ship on the ocean. If viewed from the shore, the ship looks calm and still, regardless of the waves around it.

Single Parenthood

Being a single parent is, today, a regular occurrence. Very often, there is another parent in the picture, but this second parent may not be living in the same home. Even if you're in a situation like this, it's still important to model appropriate interaction between yourself and this other parent. You may not love them anymore, you may not be fond of them at all, but it's imperative that your child is not put in the middle of your negative relationship.

Insulting the other parent and name-calling is not appropriate for your child to hear. Remember, you may have a problem with your ex-partner, but this is still your child's parent, and they still love them and share a bond.

— Dating

As a single parent, if you choose to date, you'll be role modeling in this area, too. But before you go on a date, think about what you would expect from your child if they were the one going out with a suitor. Would you expect them to come home at a reasonable hour? Is there a number where they can reach you if there's a problem?

If you're approach is heading out for the night and not returning until the next morning, then you should expect similar behavior from your child when they're old enough to date. Or, if you're always dating different people, don't be surprised if your teen follows this dating style and plays the field.

Be aware that your actions will play a part in how your children determine what's acceptable or unacceptable in the world of dating.

Role Modeling Abusive Relationships

Just like a positive relationship, negative relationships are also observed by our impressionable children. Echoing the cycle of poverty, the cycle of abuse often repeats generation after generation.

Specifically, if a man is abusive towards his wife, he's teaching his son how to treat women and showing his daughter what to expect from a man. There's a strong chance that the son will become abusive towards women, even his own mother, and that the daughter may subconsciously seek out a man who will one day be abusive towards her. This is what these children are familiar with; this is what they know.

For women in abusive relationships, they may think they should stay and "do the right thing" for their kids, or that they can't leave. Unfortunately, for many who do escape a household of abuse, they'll often find another relationship with the same abusive tendencies—it is simply the type of relationship both sides are familiar with, and it's difficult to end this painful cycle.

However, while an abused spouse may have a very difficult time getting out, it's crucial to understand the repercussions of what you're role modeling for your kids. If a mother is in an abusive relationship, allowing a man to be physically or verbally abusive, she's role modeling that this type of behavior is acceptable to her daughter. Actions speak louder than words, so no matter how many times she tells her daughter to avoid this type of relationship, this is what she's seeing as an example of acceptable dating/marriage.

~ Tick Tock …

Picture the abusive cycle like a clock, where a "blow up" or violence takes place at the top of the hour. As the hand moves around, there is begging for forgiveness and the giving of gifts, such as flowers or candy. Then, as the hand continues to move around, frustration begins to build again, and angry words start to come out, until the next explosion at the top of the next hour.

So, by taking the initiative to leave an abusive relationship, you'll be helping not only yourself, but your children, too. The choice to leave will have a great impact on the direction your children will take when they're older. This is an important area to get counseling in before you enter into a new relationship.

— Did you know?

Many remember the incident in early 2009, when a famous couple got into a fight on the way to a music awards ceremony. In a nutshell, a famous R&B singer used his pop-star girlfriend as a punching bag. The story was salaciously covered in the media.

However, what was more shocking than this outrageous display of dating violence were the results of a survey conducted by the Boston Public Health Commission following the incident. Though only a small sample was surveyed, 200 youths from the Boston area, aged 12–19, the implications of the results are disturbing: *46%* of the teens said the woman (who was beaten severely enough to require hospital treatment) was *"responsible"* for the incident!

The end result: the man pleaded guilty and was sentenced to community service and probation. Not much of a consequence for such a violent act—what message does that send to our children?

Modeling Effective Communication

Communication is another skill and technique that we model for our children on a daily basis. Listening, questioning, clarifying, and conveying thoughts are learned behaviors. If Mom or Dad never listens when the other is speaking, their children will also likely be poor listeners when they communicate with others. On the other hand, if the parents model what a good listener is by conversing politely, then their kids will be able to mimic and model this behavior correctly.

Additionally, communication is a key element in dealing with potential conflict. For instance, if Mom doesn't like conflict, yet prefers a passive aggressive approach, the child will likely adopt a similar style to dealing with conflict. However, if situations are addressed head on, with assertiveness, clearly expressing thoughts and feelings, our children will instead use these skills when faced with a similar situation.

Anger Management

Just like communication, how we deal with anger and manage our feelings of frustration will act as a set of guidelines for our children about how to handle their own feelings. If you lose control, you're very likely to see your child lose control when confronted with those same emotions. We can't expect our children to act any differently than we do.

For example, if you're driving in the family car with kids in tow and somebody cuts you off—if you start cursing and yelling, you should expect to see your kids react the same way when they get behind the wheel of the car.

Therefore, it's paramount that we learn to handle our feelings of anger and frustration appropriately. That way, we'll be able to show our kids suitable ways to work through these feelings. Your behavior is going to play a big part in how your kids act and react in stressful situations.

Appropriate Actions & Reactions

Role modeling is crucial to the healthy development of a child. For instance, if a child is continually faced with inappropriate and strange behavior, they may soon start to believe that this is normal. Consider a healthy child who is raised by a schizophrenic mother—this child would have a very high chance of adopting many of her schizophrenic behaviors and tendencies because this mother would be a key role model in their life. The child will be influenced by these interactions, dialogues, and witness to the mother's reactions.

Imagine this mother opening her arms to her child, signaling that she wants to give them a hug. The child walks over to the mother for the hug, yet she suddenly pushes them away, saying, "Get away from me. Why are you so clingy?" With this type of mixed message, the child becomes confused and often believes they've misunderstood or done something wrong.

For better or worse, our kids will mimic our behavior. So, if a parent doesn't take care of themselves, they'll likely pass on that trait, whether they want to or not.

Religion

Regardless of your beliefs, if you claim to follow a religion, it's important to model this consistently for your children. For instance, some people may say they follow a certain religion, yet their whole lifestyle is inconsistent with this claim. Instead, strive to have your actions match what you say your beliefs are.

Furthermore, if religion is something you value, it's crucial that you introduce this practice early on in your child's life. Take your child to church, synagogue, or other place of worship regularly and have them be a part of this practice. It goes without saying, but it's much easier to initiate this type of activity and establish these beliefs when your child is young, rather than starting when they're out of control and sixteen years old. Chances are, if you try to begin when they're teenagers, your kids won't be very receptive to these new ideas and practices.

This is not to say that you should "brainwash" your child and try to limit what they can and cannot do explicitly. It's actually okay if your kids even question what they're hearing from the pastor, priest, or rabbi, etc. But by consistently role modeling these values, beliefs, and faith, you're exposing your child to an authentic look at the religion as opposed to just the rhetoric.

You'll also be giving them the opportunity to genuinely absorb these teachings, instead of turning to them as a last resort when they're in trouble. If you only talk about these beliefs, but your kids don't really experience them, they'll be more likely to gravitate towards the actions, ethics, and beliefs of their peers rather than the ones you're trying to encourage at home.

Modeling Hobbies & Habits

We also model our hobbies and habits for our children; exposing them to our likes, dislikes, addictions, and aversions. This includes everything from sports, arts, outdoor pursuits, and games, but also smoking, drinking, pornography, and gambling.

As discussed in previous chapters, exposure to pornography can have an adverse effect on young children and adolescents. However, this means that as a male role model, you shouldn't leave pornographic magazines around the house. While this may be one of your "personal interests," your children, daughters and sons alike, should not be aware of it. Exposure to porn simply leads kids down a path they're not ready to go down.

Similarly, gambling is another pastime that many people have. Whether it's playing the lottery, online poker, slot machines, or betting on sporting events, it can be particularly dangerous, as it's become a socially-acceptable hobby. However, if you choose to gamble, and I'm not saying you should or shouldn't, understand that you are modeling this activity for your children.

Just like smoking, drinking, and pornography, gambling is an activity not suited for children. Yet, if it is demonstrated repeatedly in front of youngsters, they will take an interest in it. For example, I've worked with teens who are playing dice in high school during their lunch hour, gambling with lunch money, and others who are beaten up if they don't pay the money owed.

As an adult, these habits are personal choices, but be wary about which ones you model for your children; it can be a slippery slope once they get hooked, as these behaviors are very addictive.

Case in Point: Alcoholism

A friend of mine grew up with an abusive, alcoholic father. Throughout his childhood, he saw his father drink and he was generally fearful of him, as the alcohol made his father unpredictable.

Though his father would never let him drink, on the day of his twenty-first birthday the young man walked right up to his dad and popped open a can of beer, drinking it down, much to the dismay of his father.

He could see the anger in his father's eyes, but knew that there was nothing his dad could say; after all, his dad had been drinking and getting drunk for the young man's entire life. This is the behavior the father had been modeling for his son all these years.

Basically, we can't tell our kids one thing, and then do another. Regardless of what we say, they will be inclined to emulate our actions, not our words.

> ### ~ Grandkids
>
> The way you parent your kids will largely influence how they will parent your future grandkids. In other words, how you treat your kids is a good indication of how they will interact with their children. Of course, at that stage, when you're a grandparent, it's unlikely that you'll have much input into that matter.

Family Time

Role modeling family time together is a good strategy to help keep your children on the right path. Eating a meal together as a family is a great pattern to get into, as it encourages all members of the family to stay connected. It also gives everyone a chance to discuss what's going on in their life.

If this seems like a challenge, pick one meal time and make this a family priority. Try starting this habit when your kids are young, then as they get older, eating dinner together will be the norm instead of a rare occasion. If it becomes part of everyone's routine, "We always sit down together for dinner and talk," then you'll be on the right track from day one.

I realize that many parents want to make these changes in reaction to a family crisis, or a child who's acting out that needs more structure, but try being pre-emptive and establish this positive, healthy routine from early on. This way, if your child is going through something challenging, as a family you've established this routine of daily communication.

Prioritize this time together, and show your kids that this is a priority for you.

Cats in the Cradle

When I think about role modeling, I'm always reminded of the 1970s song "Cat's in the Cradle" by Harry Chapin and Sandra Chapin. The song tells the story of a father who never has time for his son while he's growing up. Despite this, the son is always saying that he wants to be just like his dad.

At the end of the song, the son has grown up and the father is now looking to spend time with him. Unfortunately, the tables have turned and now the son doesn't have time to spend with his dad; the father then realizes that his boy grew up to be just like him.

Cat's in the Cradle
by Harry Chapin and Sandra Chapin

My child arrived just the other day
Came to the world in the usual way
But there were planes to catch and bills to pay
He learned to walk while I was away
He was talkin' 'fore I knew it
And as he grew he said,
"I'm gonna be like you, Dad,
You know I'm gonna be like you."

Chorus
And the cat's in the cradle and the silver spoon,
Little boy blue and the man 'n the moon.
"When you comin' home?"
"Son, I don't know when. We'll get together then.
You know we'll have a good time then."

Well, my son turned ten just the other day.
He said, "Thanks for the ball, Dad. Come on, let's play.
Could you teach me to throw?"
I said, "Not today. I got a lot to do."
He said, "That's okay." And he walked away and he smiled and he said,
"You know, I'm gonna be like him, yeah.
You know I'm gonna be like him."

Chorus

Well, he came from college just the other day,
So much like a man I just had to say,
"I'm proud of you. Could you sit for a while?"
He shook his head and he said with a smile,
"What I'd really like, Dad, is to borrow the car keys.
See you later. Can I have them please?"

Chorus

I've long since retired, my son's moved away.
I called him up just the other day.
"I'd like to see you, if you don't mind."
He said, "I'd love to, Dad, if I could find the time.
You see my new job's a hassle and the kids have the flu,
But it's sure nice talkin' to you, Dad.
It's been sure nice talkin' to you."
And as I hung up the phone it occurred to me,
He'd grown up just like me.
My boy was just like me.

9 Taking Care of Yourself

Though easy to overlook, an important part of parenting is actually taking care of ourselves as individuals. Simply put, if you're not taking care of yourself, you're not in a suitable frame of mind or physical health, to be the best parent you can be.

Overworked, overtired, emotionally drained, frustrated in your marriage, or physically out of shape; these are not qualities any of us would consider beneficial in the role of parenting.

So, it's important that we make time to take the necessary steps to reach a healthy lifestyle—emotionally, physically, and in your relationships with others. These positive adjustments can help you on a personal level, as well as help your children. After all, problems in any of these areas are bound to spill over and start to affect our kids, sooner or later. For instance, a frustrated mother may overreact to a child's mistake; a disengaged Dad might not recognize his child's ongoing need for his attention and affection; all because they haven't taken care of themselves.

Remember—helping yourself is being a good mom or dad. You're not being selfish, but instead ensuring that you're in the best position to be a good parent to your children.

Staying Active

Being physically active is something I recommend to everyone. Unless instructed by your doctor otherwise, almost all adults (and children) can benefit from thirty minutes of daily physical activity. It can be going for a walk, playing tennis, shooting hoops, golfing, or even going for a bike ride. No matter what the activity, exercise helps us feel better both on a physical and an emotional level.

Basically, an increased activity level will help boost your metabolism, which may help you maintain a healthy weight. Additionally, regular exercise is known for its overall positive effects on your body's wellness—helping your heart, lungs, muscles, etc., in addition to promoting an active mind.

Furthermore, exercise helps us emotionally; by prioritizing time each day to keep fit, you're also prioritizing thirty minutes to spend on yourself. Plus, while exercising, you'll have this time to restore balance and focus on yourself, decreasing your personal stress and improving your own emotional health.

As mentioned above, if you're concerned about spending this time away from your family, think again. How much more will you be able to do for your family if you're fit and in a balanced emotional state? Plus, if you choose, you can include your kids or your spouse in these activities.

In fact, exercise is a great pastime to enjoy with your partner. Together, you can use this time to stay connected as a couple. If this is an option, find an activity that you both enjoy doing, or alternate between your interest and theirs.

Regardless of the well-known benefits of exercise, many people still don't make time for it. Instead of waiting until you "feel like" exercising, make this daily activity part of your routine. Make a decision to exercise every day. Tell yourself: it doesn't matter if you feel like it or not, you will go for a walk today. Once you've been active for about three weeks straight, you may find yourself enjoying it and even wanting to exercise!

When Times are Tough

Despite these activities that can help our overall wellness, at one point or another, we all need someone we can lean on when we're having a difficult time. This may be a spouse or a close friend, and sometimes it might even be helpful to confide in a therapist. Though it's still perceived as a sign of weakness by some, seeking professional help to work though an issue is in fact a sign of strength.

Sometimes parents may benefit from talking to someone outside of friends and family. Even if it's simply talking to a counselor for a few sessions, seeking professional input can be a great help. In most cases, you'll take away new skills and techniques depending on your needs, whether it's learning to be more assertive or coping strategies for a difficult time.

Although, remember—as one person grows and develops, other members of the household may find these changes difficult and may even be unsupportive of any personal progress. In a way, by changing or growing, you've change the rules of the relationship, so your partner and/or children may initially be confused and negative. So, in a perfect world, both you and your partner need to be involved in the process as part of the change.

By dealing with a concern or problem head on, with any of these suitable and appropriate people, we can lessen the chance of burdening and unloading our problems onto our children. Take a minute to identify who this supportive person is in your life, and if they're not there, take the necessary steps to fill that supportive role.

~ Forgive the Past

Most people have made a choice or done something that they later regret. If you've made poor choices in the past, don't condemn yourself forever or dwell on the thought that you're a bad person—nothing really gets accomplished by that. Learn from these mistakes and move forward.

Aggressive, Assertive, Passive

Part of taking care of yourself is being able to stand up for yourself. When someone is able to stand up for themselves, talk about how they actually feel, what they think and express themselves regarding their priorities; this can be defined as an *assertive* person.

Of course, being assertive is the ideal middle ground, however, there are those parents on the two extremes of this perspective—those who are aggressive and those who are passive.

An *aggressive* person is usually seen as angry, or even confrontational, whereas a *passive* person tends to accept whatever situation they find themselves in and often allows others to take advantage of them.

Between these two extremes is assertiveness—a trait worth striving for.

— How do I come across?

Do others see you as an aggressive, assertive, or passive person? If you're not sure, first consider how you see yourself.

If there's a problem with a co-worker, how do you react? Do you:

a) React immediately, demanding and arguing your point of view until all parties agree;

b) Stand up for yourself and express your point, while listening to and considering the thoughts of others;

c) Meekly follow along, staying out of the discussion, and putting up with whatever is decided, even if you disagree?

Answers a, b, and c, are aggressive, assertive, and passive reactions, respectively. If you're still unsure though, try asking your partner. Use the communication skills discussed at the beginning of this book, and ask for their honest feedback. Then, listen to their comments. If they say: "You seem angry all the time," think about whether this matches your own view of yourself. If it doesn't, maybe there are underlying issues that you need to deal with, so they don't reveal themselves in inappropriate or unfortunate ways. This might mean trying some of the anger management strategies discussed in this chapter, such as writing exercises or relaxation techniques, or it could mean seeking help from a counselor or psychologist.

~ Do Opposites Attract?

In my opinion, the age-old saying is both true and false. Many times an aggressive person will seek out a passive person for a mate and vice versa—so, on the surface this saying appears true. However, underneath either of these extreme façades, one usually finds very similar underlying issues, e.g., beneath the surface, each person may actually feel insecure.

> Therefore, although a couple appears to be opposites, they are in fact quite similar. One may shy away and be passive due to feelings of insecurity, while the other may overcompensate and be aggressive, in an attempt to feel more powerful, because they too lack confidence in themselves.

A true example of opposites would be a person who has their life together and a person with a life that's out of control. These opposites seldom attract.

Empty Nest Syndrome

Many parents find it difficult when their children leave the family home and move out on their own for the first time. And it's easy to see why. For the eighteen+ years leading up to this moment, your children have been the center of your world; all the way through, you've been there supporting and encouraging them. Then, suddenly it seems, your kids are heading off to college, getting married, and leaving home. This exodus can leave many parents with a sense that there's nothing left.

One of the reasons behind this feeling of emptiness is due to the fact that when our children are at home, so much of our lives is wrapped up in their lives. You may have spent the last ten years being a soccer mom or a dad who coaches the baseball team, so it may be difficult for these familiar routines and activities to suddenly disappear.

However, there are many proactive things that we can do as parents to help this eventual reality of an "empty nest" not feel as difficult for us. In short, it's all about balance—we need to be involved in our children's lives (as I've suggested throughout this book) yet we shouldn't become so wrapped up in them that we have no life of our own.

If your whole world is taking care of your children, then you're bound to have a very uneasy time when they leave. So, instead of dedicating your entire life to them, strike a balance between being an active, engaged parent, and a well-rounded, healthy individual. By achieving this balance, you'll be in a better, stronger position to deal with the feelings that come with future change.

— Swallowing your feelings

A common reaction and coping strategy for parents dealing with Empty Nest syndrome is seeking comfort in food, or "swallowing your feelings," which often results in overeating and unhealthy food choices.

The good news is that by simply recognizing the warning signs, you can stop yourself from falling into this familiar pitfall. For instance, if you're entering an Empty Nest transition, you may find yourself wanting to eat more, sitting around for longer periods of time, and even making poor dietary decisions. Now, though, you're in a position to anticipate these impulses and urges, so you can act accordingly. You'll be saying: "I was expecting this, so I'm not going to swallow my feelings."

Additionally, if this is an ongoing issue for you, try cutting out the root of the problem by making healthier choices in the grocery store. If you buy fruits and vegetables when shopping instead of potato chips and ice cream, then you won't be tempted by unhealthy snack foods when you're feeling low.

At the end of the day, most people won't go out and buy unhealthy food to eat because they're unhappy—we usually eat whatever is in the cupboard/fridge. Yet, if it's there, it can be quite tempting to grab the unhealthy snacks and munch away. Therefore, planning ahead and being proactive can help greatly when you find yourself eating to suppress your emotions.

— The next chapter in your life

Try changing your perspective. Look at your empty nest as a new opportunity or the next chapter in your life. With a clearer schedule and less people at home, you'll likely have time to take on a hobby or start a new adventure. See this as an opportunity to try something you've always been interested in learning, but too busy to start.

Maybe you've always wanted to learn how to play tennis, or to paint, write poetry, take a pottery class, improve your gardening skills; the sky's the limit! View this new chapter as a chance to do something for yourself. Take a personal interest class at your local college or get involved in a community project.

An empty nest needn't be a negative period in your life, but a positive one. Instead of feeling like: "The kids are gone, now what?" try thinking: "The kids are gone, now I can do this...."

You have a chance to finally do some of those things you wanted to do in the past, but that maybe didn't fit with everything else that was going on. Enjoy yourself!

— Pursue your own life

Another great proactive strategy for dealing with Empty Nest syndrome is to maintain an outside life, apart from your children—with your partner, your friends, your job, etc. These aspects are all part of a normal life, and by including them in yours, you may find it easier to adjust during this transition period.

Consider the parent who has a few close friends, volunteers with a local community group, and has always prioritized "Friday night date night" with her husband. Then, consider the mom who has dedicated her entire life to her children—everything she does from the moment she gets up in the morning is related to the well-being of her kids. Which parent will have an easier time adjusting when her children leave home? Again, it's an issue of balance: prioritize your kids, but take some time for yourself, too.

— Socializing

Part of having your own life is fostering friendships with others. If you currently don't have many friends, you may need to reach out and make time to pursue new friendships and develop connections with people that are your own age.

Even if you're introverted and find making friends a challenge, it doesn't mean you can't try. Yes, you'll need to step outside of your comfort zone, but this is good for everybody to do once in a while. Of course, the more we do a new activity, the more comfortable we become with it; our comfort zone expands accordingly.

Additionally, by having this support system in place, you may find it a bit easier when your kids leave home, because you'll already have ongoing activities and friends in place.

— Don't live vicariously through your kids

Did you know: people often use their kids as a means of escaping their life? A parent who is overly involved in their child may be using their youngster as a way to avoid dealing with their own issues. The adult may be trying to avoid doing things on their own, or they're seeking an escape from their personal challenges. Also, they may be afraid to experience life by themselves; or they may encourage their kids to pursue the dreams they never accomplished.

However, using your child's life as an escape is not the answer. Be proactive and get involved in your own life now. Don't live vicariously through your children, but instead role model for them a healthy balance of taking care of yourself, while taking care of them. Being a good parent is not about sacrificing your life entirely and dedicating 100% of your time to your children. This doesn't make you a great parent. Instead, show your kids that you're a responsible adult, leading a productive life.

Your kids certainly need to be a major priority, but they're not 100% of your life. Therefore, try making any adjustments before your children leave home; that way, when the time comes, all of these steps will make this empty nest transition much easier.

Connect with Your Partner*

It's vital that you maintain an engaged and fulfilling relationship with your spouse. Together, the two of you need to take care of your relationship. Each one of you needs to make an effort and prioritize your "love," even when your children are still at home. Although, many of us put our marital relationships on hold while raising the kids, once these children have left home, you may find yourselves trying to rekindle your marriage and needing to get to know your spouse all over again.

"We just don't know each other," is a common sentiment I hear from couples when they find themselves sharing a house together, without kids, for the first time in decades. Instead of this reality, it's important to keep the fires burning in your relationship throughout the years.

Of course, if this seems challenging, start with something like a scheduled "date night." Make Friday night (or Saturday) at 8 p.m., your time together. Get a babysitter and spend some time, just the two of you connecting together, sharing and learning what's going on in your lives.

You don't have to feel guilty about taking this time for each other. You should have set aside time to be available for your children, and now this is the time you've each set aside to spend with your partner. You need this time together to continue to build and maintain your relationship, so that when your kids do leave, you don't find yourself with a stranger in your home. Instead, you can look forward to spending more quality time together as a couple.

*** Note:*** *Parts of this chapter are directed to those parents in a relationship with a partner/spouse. If you're not in that situation, these may not all be applicable to you.*

— Develop common interests

Date night is only the beginning. Strive to be involved in activities that both you and your partner enjoy doing together. It's easy to forget while our children are at home, but the majority of your adult life will not be spent raising kids. It's normal that they will be your focus for the time they're at home, but once they've left, there are likely still many years ahead in your life. Having a connection and sharing activities with your partner will make it easier for the two of you to enjoy this next phase of your life.

— Validate your mate

In any relationship, it's crucial to let your partner know that they are important to you. However, this becomes even more significant with the arrival of a new baby, when the man may feel left out, even ignored by his partner, as she is preoccupied with the baby. Even at this busy time, you need to let your man know that he is valued, too. We all need to hear this validation every now and then, so don't be afraid to tell your spouse how you feel about them.

This doesn't mean you need to spend every minute of the day reassuring your partner, but you may want to try doing something small for them, every day, to let them know you care.

It can be simple. Try writing them a note, picking a flower, running them a bath, giving them a massage, making them dinner, or any little gesture that you know they'll appreciate.

If you're not sure what your partner would like—ask them! Take some time together to sit down and each write a list of ten things that you would like your partner to do for you. Focus on thoughtful everyday ways that your partner could show you their love, but don't make a list of extravagant requests like a diamond necklace, or courtside tickets to the basketball game.

Once your list is written, exchange papers. Now, you'll both know a few ways you can show your partner you're thinking of them and how special they are to you.

— Parent against parent

As discussed in earlier chapters, we shouldn't ever let children play one parent against the other. However, as parents, we need to remember this is still the case, even as our kids get older. Adult children can still split a couple down the middle in certain situations.

As a couple, there shouldn't be any secrets in your relationship, especially as far as kids are concerned. Your children need to know that Mom and Dad don't keep secrets from each other, so this type of "strategy" won't work.

For example, when your child is older, perhaps an adult themselves, they might come to you asking for money. If your spouse doesn't want to give it to them but you do, try to come to a resolution between the two of you, and then let your child know the verdict. Resist telling your child, "Here's some money—just don't tell your mother/father that I gave it to you." This type of action builds distrust in your relationship with your spouse.

Remember, your kids are going to leave home, have their own families, and you'll be continuing a relationship with your spouse. It's important to treat them with respect as this will be your partner for the rest of your lives, ideally. Thus, you need to have an open, trusting relationship.

— Have a sex life

While it may seem like common sense, many married couples become stuck in a rut and even become disinterested in their sex life as the years roll by. But being intimate with your partner is an important part of your relationship; both people need to put forth an effort in keeping the intimacy alive and exciting.

If your sex life could do with a boost, think about experimenting a little in the bedroom. Share your fantasy with your partner, or try something new. Bring excitement back into your love life, in ways both of you are comfortable with.

I realize that many people have taboos about sex—even in a marriage, one partner may find the topic difficult to discuss. Many have preconceived ideas that sex is dirty, or even wrong, and these opinions can be difficult to change. But, challenge yourself to try; intimacy is a big part of your marriage, so keep it fresh and fun.

Also, keep in mind that if you talk about sex and play with your partner in the bedroom, they'll be less likely to seek this excitement elsewhere. Ask them what they enjoy and share what you'd like to try. You may even suggest a weekend getaway, for just the two of you, in order to reconnect sexually.

Remember though, that many of us feel vulnerable while talking about sex and being intimate. Both parties need to enjoy and feel comfortable with the experience. So, if one person really wants to try something but the other person is not comfortable with it, respect that choice and do not force them into it. Instead, try something else. It's paramount that you respect your partner's boundaries and keep what happens in the bedroom as a private matter. Think of it as: "What happens in the bedroom, stays in the bedroom."

Ultimately, keep intimacy alive in your marriage, before you have children, while your kids are at home, and finally when the kids leave. Even though your kids won't know details of your sex life, you'll be role modeling what a happy and fulfilled marriage looks like.

— End result

As you work together with your partner to stay connected, you're both putting forth an effort to get beyond the superficial and come to a greater understanding of each other. You'll be moving past the small talk to get to know what's really going on inside them; this makes for a much more rewarding relationship and much deeper connection. Together, you're creating and maintaining a strong partnership that will go the distance.

Managing Your Emotions

Most people feel angry or frustrated from time to time. And as parents, we too, can feel this way, even with our children. While these feelings are okay and even normal, it's important that we deal with our emotions in an appropriate, constructive, and non-threatening way. Below, I've included some helpful strategies, as well as more general relaxation techniques to try. You may find that by practicing these relaxation exercises, your patience level will increase and stress level decrease—leaving you with fewer feelings of frustration, and more even-tempered.

— Time out

Although we've talked about time outs for our children, not all parents think of using them for themselves. For a parent, you may find that taking a time out is helpful in several different situations. For example, if you're feeling overwhelmed, stressed out, or angry with your spouse or children, take a quick fifteen-minute break from the situation and remove yourself from the stimulus.

Just like with your children, this time will give you a chance to think about the situation before you react or respond in a way you might later regret. You can make this decision ahead of time: "If I feel myself getting upset— breathing faster, heart rate increasing (or other physical symptoms)—I'm going to walk away and take a time out." You can even pre-arrange a code word that lets your spouse or children know that you need a time out.

Once you're away from the stimulation, there are several things you can do to help calm yourself down—exercise, deep breathing, guided imagery, meditation, and writing.

— Exercise

An effective way to work through feelings of anger and frustration is through exercise. This method works on two levels: chemical and physical. First, when you exercise your body releases endorphins, which on an internal level make you feel better emotionally. On a physical level, exercise will help your body vent this built up energy, so instead of it coming out as anger, this adrenaline can be used towards a physical activity, such as running or doing push-ups.

> ### ~ Fight or Flight
>
> When angry or stressed, our body may react as if we're in a life-or-death situation. It may automatically rev up your internal systems and switch over to the sympathetic nervous system—your heart starts racing, you're breathing faster, blood vessels in your hands and feet start to constrict, and your body basically prepares itself to either fight, protecting itself, or to flee. And if you were in a life-or-death situation, your body would need this adrenaline rush. However, this same physical, non-voluntary reaction can also be triggered when you get angry at your children or spouse.

So, you're frustrated and angry at the situation at home, and your body has switched into fight-or-flight mode. Now what? There isn't anything to run away from, and you don't want to get into a physical altercation with your loved ones, but you still need to release this energy.

In this case, take a time out and physically use up the energy through exercise. For example, when you're feeling angry, go to your room and do 100 push-ups. You can take a break, but you can't leave the room until you've done 100.

In essence, you need to use this adrenaline and energy in a constructive way, as exercise is a much better option than acting out inappropriately with your family or bottling up these feelings inside. It's important to note that holding onto these emotions and issues can result in medical problems down the road, such as high blood pressure, stomach ulcers, heart disease, etc. The simple solution—let it out!

— Breathing as a way to relax

Another way to stop this fight-or-flight response is to help your body relax and convince it that there is no imminent threat. However, it's not just a matter of wanting to calm down; your body actually needs physical cues to restore itself back to a normal state, and back to using the parasympathetic nervous system. When this happens, your heart rate and breathing rate slows down, your blood vessels open up again, so your hands and feet feel warmer—a chain reaction occurs in your body, resulting in a relaxed state. But how can you influence this change from one nervous system to the other, from fight-or-flight to relaxed?

You need to trigger one of these physical indicators, which in turn will tell the rest of your body that the "crisis" is over. While many of the physical cues are difficult to control, there is one factor that is easy to influence and manipulate—your breathing rate. And, once you set this in motion, the rest of the physical signs of anger and stress will switch back and return to a calm state.

Here is an exercise I recommend which, when used in a stressed state, will help to bring your body back to a normal state, and when used regularly will encourage a sense of relaxation:

To begin—lie down on your back, with one hand on your stomach.

You're going to practice deep breathing, taking deep breaths using your diaphragm.

Now, slowly breathe in, to the count of 5; 1-2-3-4-5

Completely fill your lungs with air and feel your hand rise on your abdomen.

Then, hold your breath to the count of 4; 1-2-3-4

And, breathe out very slowly, counting to 7. As you breathe out, focus in your mind on the word "calm." Stretch the word out, as you exhale slowly—"ca---lm."

Now, try doing ten sets of this breathing exercise—10 full breaths.

While it may sound silly, you'll be surprised at how refreshed, focused and calm you feel once finished. Many people almost fall asleep by the end of it, or notice their hands feeling much warmer. These are all your body's physical cues telling you that it's now relaxed. This is a perfect technique to use in any stressful situation; in a matter of minutes, you'll be able to calm yourself down. After a while, you'll be able to use this skill anywhere.

— Guided imagery

Guided imagery is another helpful technique to try when you're feeling stressed, overwhelmed, or you simply want to escape for a few minutes. This method of relaxation is straightforward and easy to do on your own.

To begin—lie down, and close your eyes.

You're going to work from your toes all the way to your head, tensing and relaxing each set of muscles as you go.

Start with your toes. Tense the muscles in your toes and feet, holding this tension as tight as you can, while you slowly count to 10. Then release these muscles in your feet. Feel how relaxed these muscles now are.

Next, move to your calf muscles. Tighten these muscles and hold it. Again, slowly count to 10, keeping as much tension as possible, then release. Enjoy the relaxation that you now feel in these calf muscles.

Continue this pattern of tension and relaxation. Tense the muscles in your thighs, in your hips, in your stomach, your chest, and your back. Continue with your shoulders, your arms, your hands (make a fist), your jaw (clench your jaw), your face and eyes (furrow your brow, make a frown).

By intentionally introducing tension to each of these muscles groups, you're forcing them to relax—because they often won't just relax on their own, but they'll naturally want to let go after this prolonged period of tension.

This exercise is very effective, as many people carry a tremendous amount of tension in their jaws and shoulders. Through this exercise, you'll be able to notice what relaxation in these areas feels like, so that hopefully you'll become aware and notice when you're feeling tension in these bodily zones. Being able to tell the difference between tension and relaxation will help you address these issues promptly.

The guided imagery part of this exercise follows:

Now that your body is relaxed, picture yourself in a peaceful setting. Somewhere you can simply let go and be alone. Maybe you're on the beach—there's nobody on the sand but you; perhaps you're sitting on top of a mountain, gazing into the distance. For someone else, a peaceful setting may be lying in a field of wildflowers, or sitting on the edge of a forest, watching a river run by.

Wherever you find yourself, picture yourself calm and alone. Now, using your five senses (sight, sound, taste, touch, and smell) make your peaceful place come alive. What can you see when you look around? (Are there clouds in the sky? What's in the distance?) Do you hear anything? (Birds chirping? Water rushing?) What does the air smell like? (Salt water? Wild flowers?) What can you feel around you? (The warm sand through your fingers? The soft grass all around you?)

Take a few minutes and think about this image—bring yourself to this peaceful location. If it helps, think of this like a mini-vacation, where you can get away from everything for a few minutes.

— Meditation

Similar to deep breathing and guided imagery, meditation focuses on calming your body and mind, beginning with focused breathing. Traditionally, however, the goal of meditation is to let your mind go totally blank; as well, there are other techniques where you focus on a single phrase or word.

This is a more challenging exercise, as it can be difficult to clear your mind, but still, meditation is worth trying and practicing.

> *To begin—sit in a comfortable position with your back straight, and close your eyes. Focus on breathing in and out, slowly, calmly.*
>
> *Gradually feel yourself letting go of the day's concerns, issues and problems. If something comes into your mind, acknowledge the thought, and then let it go, gently pushing the thought out of your mind. If you find your mind wandering, try focusing on a word, such as "calm" or "peace," or your favorite scripture, and repeat this to yourself.*

Unlike the first two relaxation techniques, meditation does take time to master. You may need to practice many times before you're able to actually let your mind go totally blank. Nevertheless, when you're able to accomplish this, the effect can be extremely relaxing, even rejuvenating.

~ Practice!

Everyone can benefit from practicing these relaxation techniques—there are no adverse side effects! Even if you're feeling fine, take a break and try one of them. After all, who wouldn't enjoy ten minutes of peacefulness and calmness in today's busy world. Also, by practicing these skills when you're not in a stressful situation, they will be much more effective when you are stressed. For instance, if you're feeling road rage, you can practice some deep breathing at the stop light. But, practice first, and learn these techniques before you need them for the best results.

— Writing

Finally, another effective way to work through feelings of frustration and anger is to write out your emotions on paper. Even if you dislike writing, or feel silly doing it, consider this effective technique as an ongoing way to process and handle a rough period in your life. In most situations, I recommend setting aside fifteen minutes a day for two weeks, to write out how you're feeling and describe what you're going through.

You might think, "But I know how I'm feeling, so why do I need to write it?" Well, in the process of putting pen to paper and physically writing out what's going on in your head, most people find they're able to reflect and come to a greater understanding of what they're dealing with. You may even be surprised by what starts coming out. The act of writing is a way of releasing your emotions and letting go of these thoughts and feelings. You may even feel a sense of resolution with the issue at hand.

It's a very successful technique, and most people who try it find it very helpful. So, even if it seems like work, make the effort to actually sit down and write—and write for 10–15 minutes. No one needs to see what you're writing; when you're done you can save it and file it away, or just tear it up and throw it out. Either way, if you're going through a difficult time, try writing about it.

— Count to 10

If you feel yourself getting upset or even overreacting to a situation when you don't have a lot of time to calm down, simply take a deep breath and slowly count to 10. Give yourself a break from the situation and a chance to think before you react. Even just taking this minute or two can help you regroup your thoughts and think about how you'd like to respond—what is the problem, what would be the best way to react, how should I handle this?

Sometimes counting to 10 can be the difference between escalating a situation and calmly dealing with a problem. Ultimately, by remaining in control of our anger and emotions, we best convey our true thoughts and feelings to those around us in an appropriate manner.

Respecting Yourself = Respecting Your Children

At the end of the day, everything comes back to respect—demonstrating respect for yourself and your children. As a parent, if you respect yourself, you should be making choices that actively reflect this—taking time out for personal activities, working on your marriage, making balanced choices; striving to be healthy on an emotional and physical level.

By respecting yourself, you'll be role modeling this self-respect for your child. Furthermore, you'll also be parenting from an improved perspective, which will likely result in a more respectful, even-handed approach in all areas.

Therefore, instead of "sacrificing" everything for your kids, try leading a life where you respect yourself, in addition to respecting your children.

10 Conclusion

When we talk about the scope and role of parenting, it can be difficult to picture the overall goals and purpose. This is a job that spans decades, with constantly changing demands and unpredictable crises.

However, I often liken our role as parents to that classic scene of Mom or Dad teaching their youngster how to ride a bike. At the start, the parent helps their child, holding onto the bike seat—they need us there and feel safe because we're next to them.

As a parent, you're called upon to support your child, protect them, and guide them, pushing your children forward, acting as a balancing force while they're riding along. Eventually though, when we think our kids can do it on their own, we stop holding on to the bike seat, letting them ride ahead independently.

Many children look back, thinking that Mom or Dad is still holding onto the bike, and it's that precious moment when they realize that you're not holding on anymore, that they can do it on their own. This moment of success and independence mirrors the ultimate goal of parenting—to help our children be successful in life, supporting them along the way, until they can do it by themselves.

And, while learning to ride a bike may only take a few days or a few weeks, parenting is obviously a much longer task that can take a lifetime to master. Still, you'll be alongside and helping your children as they mature, keeping them on track, whether it be with education, relationships, or life in general. As parents, we need to support our children until they're able to move ahead on their own.

From developing communication skills to role modeling, from improving our discipline techniques to taking care of ourselves, there's no doubt that being a good parent takes skill, attention, and practice.

For instance, if you're trying to implement some new changes in your household, you'll need to put forward a conscious, continued effort. As with any new beginning, things may seem difficult or unusual at the start; but, remember, after a while these actions, choices, and behaviors will become more and more natural.

Just like a baby learning to walk—while the first steps will require focus, concentration, perseverance and effort—soon, these actions will become second nature. So, never give up on yourself and your family, because changes are possible, they just take time, step by step, day by day.

And if you're worried that you can't do it, believe me—you can. Personally, I grew up the sixth of seven kids, in a family that bounced from place to place throughout my childhood. My parents had limited formal schooling; neither attended past fifth grade. We lived in poverty for much of our lives. It was an angry, hostile home to grow up in. I did have a loving mother who tried to hold things together.

Yet, at some point, I decided that this wasn't the life I wanted for myself. I made the necessary changes to stop this cycle. To begin, I went to college (unlike anyone in my family), and then graduate school. When it came to having a family of my own, I made a conscious decision not to repeat the same behaviors I had seen while growing up. I didn't want to continue this type of legacy, and I took active steps to ensure that my children grew up in a warm, safe, and respectful home.

Remember to be patient with yourself and your family. As you implement changes in your home, you may not start with everyone's cooperation; after all, the status quo is changing. However, the rewards are definitely worth the effort. And don't be afraid to ask for help, whether it be friends, family, or professional help; sometimes we all need support, just like the child trying to ride his bike.

This could be the start of a new day for your family. For example, imagine

150 years from now, when a future ancestor is looking back at every generation in your family. For decades, your family may have had problems with gangs, violence, abuse, etc. And then suddenly, the family history changes direction—love, respect, productivity, and success have replaced the previous negative cycle. In the years that follow this turning point, this same positive cycle is repeated and repeated. This can be the generation where your family's history makes its own turning point. Your generation, right now.

Change is never easy, but you need to do it. It's in everybody's best interest to be the best parent you can be. Don't let TV parent your kids; that's the easy way out. It may take a lot of hard work, and even a long time, yet there isn't a better payoff than a happy, healthy family.

Remember, people most often reflect later in life that they wish they would have spent more time with their family while their children were still young. Very few people look back on their life, wishing they'd spent more time in the office, playing golf, working on a project, accumulating all those toys.

We can learn from this. Although it's easy to push the regular daily activities to the back burner—saying, "When I've got time, I'll spend it with you…. "—don't let this excuse come between you and your kids. Instead, prioritize your children and make the decision to spend time together; quality family time, right now.

Of course, you've already taken the brave first steps by reading *Respect Your Children*. I'd also like to encourage you to come back to this book in a month's time, or even six month's time. Take a look and see what changes have been made in your house, and identify those spots that may still need work. Remember, while certain areas may see immediate improvements, others may require much more time and effort before a difference can be seen.

Furthermore, your family's needs and concerns will change over time. So, while today there may be one area demanding your attention; a few months from now, when that situation is under control, another crisis may pop up. Also, you might identify an area where taking proactive steps would be helpful and you will be ready to face these issues head on.

Being a parent is not a popularity contest; there will be good days, but there will also be bad days. Nevertheless, don't be swayed to give in—often when we look back as adults, we appreciate the hard choices and firm direction that our parents gave us. Similarly, you may also look back and wish your parent had stepped in more, or put more emphasis on the importance of certain choices.

Regardless of what your children say at this moment, at this age—by providing structure, teaching values and role modeling respect—we'll be giving them the best foundation for the road ahead.

Therefore, as your children grow, and when you reread the book again, be sure to also redo the "Family Circles" exercise. If you kept your family's original pictures, compare them to these subsequent circles. This should give you additional insight as to how your kids view these changes in the household and your progress as a family. While you might not reach your ultimate family goal in one or even six months, this should help show you if you're on the right track.

Moreover, I hope that having read this book, you've found it helpful. But, like the old saying goes: "Don't throw the baby out with the bathwater." If there were aspects that weren't useful to you, don't get caught up in them. Be selective and use the information that is useful. If a certain area doesn't apply to your family on this particular day, then feel free to ignore for now. Just don't bundle all the information together and discard. Feel free to utilize what's currently relevant, pertinent, and beneficial to your situation.

Ultimately, these children, your kids—nothing can replace them. They are an invaluable part of your family. So, respect them, as they are certainly amongst the most important people in your life. Of course, it's natural that they may frustrate you from time to time, but the bottom line is that each one of your children is precious and unique. Treat them with the love and respect they deserve. You'll be role modeling this respectful behavior for them, and encouraging them to act with the same respect as they grow older.

As you continue on your journey, view this day as a crossroads in your life. See the turning point and make a change.

You deserve it, your kids deserve it—*respect* can be earned, given or taken away. Share it with your family.

Author's Biography

Jay Fitter is a Licensed Marriage and Family Therapist from Corona, California. He received his undergraduate degree in psychology from Hope International University and his graduate degree in family counselling from Azusa Pacific University. He was the recipient of academic awards from both schools. For the past nineteen years, he has counseled with children, adolescents and parents alike, helping them to work through their issues and improve their lives. He has worked in private practice settings and foster care, as well as juvenile detention facilities.

Jay has led numerous seminars, including recognizing and reporting child abuse for school districts, effective communication skills, and anger management/impulse control skills.

Jay has addressed a diverse range of topics in individual therapy, including parenting skills, depression, phobias, substance abuse, negative behaviors, and sexual abuse; his passion lies with helping parents create a healthy, balanced, and safe home environment for their children.

Jay has been married for twenty-one years to his wife Ann. Together, they have two sons attending the University of California, and a daughter in the seventh grade.

Having led his popular, bi-annual parenting classes in his community for several years, Jay has now completed his book, *Respect Your Children*, hoping to share his knowledge and insight with an even broader audience.

Manufactured By: RR Donnelley
                     Breinigsville, PA USA
                     April 2010